THE CONCEPT OF JUDGMENT IN MONTAIGNE

THE CONCEPT OF JUDGMENT IN MONTAIGNE

by

RAYMOND C. LA CHARITÉ

MARTINUS NIJHOFF / THE HAGUE / 1968

ISBN 978-94-015-0357-0 ISBN 978-94-015-0919-0 (eBook)
DOI 10.1007/978-94-015-0919-0

TO GINI

Nous nous cherchions avant
que de nous estre veus

TABLE OF CONTENTS

ACKNOWLEDGMENTS

I am greatly indebted to Donald M. Frame of Columbia University, under whose guidance and assistance this study was prepared, for his wonderful encouragement, his admirable patience, and his extremely valuable suggestions; but, above all, I am most grateful to him for his generosity and kindness as both professor and friend.

I also wish to thank Frank P. Bowman and Robert K. Bishop of the University of Pennsylvania for their careful reading and criticism of the manuscript.

The debt I owe my wife is immeasurable, for she made it all possible.

INTRODUCTION

Many critics seem to consider it inappropriate or unnecessary to ask what Montaigne means by the faculty of judgment. Laumonier speaks of "le *bon sens,* qu'il oppose si souvent à la mémoire et qu'il appelle encore 'jugement' et 'entendement', c'est-à-dire la faculté de penser et de réfléchir juste." [1] Our appreciation of what is implied by judgment, that is by Montaigne's notion of judgment, has been delayed perhaps by a too facile acceptance of a so-called synonymity of meaning among the psychological terms used by Montaigne. In a discussion of key concepts in Montaigne, Donald M. Frame has accurately summarized the present situation with regard to our knowledge of Montaigne's notion of judgment and other key concepts: "We all have our hunches, but we need more than that." [2]

For the expression of his interest and concern for the intellectual and moral activities and capabilities of the mind, Montaigne draws upon a broad and elementary semantic field. These primary psychological terms are *jugement, entendement, sens, raison, discours,* and *conscience.* Although these words may be used synonymously, Montaigne does seem to maintain certain basic distinctions among them; frequent substitutions of terms must be the result of semantic and ideational differences. Moreover, the association of several psychological words within a single sentence implies gradations, however slight they may be. This study represents, in part, an effort to elucidate and clarify the distinctions and relationships which exist, in Montaigne's usage, among the above-mentioned words. More importantly, this study concentrates on a detailed semantic and ideational analysis of the most significant,

[1] Paul Laumonier, "Montaigne précurseur du XVIIe siècle," *Revue d'histoire littéraire de la France,* III (1896), 209. André Cresson, *Montaigne, sa vie, son oeuvre* (Paris, 1947), p. 59, remarks that "le but doit être la formation de l'esprit, le développement de ce bon sens, de ce jugement que chacun porte en lui."

[2] Donald M. Frame, "What Next in Montaigne Studies?," *French Review,* XXXVI (1963), 583.

for both Montaigne and his reader, of these words, that is the term and concept *jugement.*[1]

The concept of judgment is central to Montaigne. Indeed, it constitutes perhaps the essential part of the odyssey for self-reliance and self-discovery which Montaigne undertakes in his *Essais*: "Le jugement est un util à tous subjects, et se mesle par tout. A cette cause, aux essais que j'en fay ici, j'y employe toute sorte d'occasion" (I, 50, 289).[2] Knowledge of the world is possible only through knowledge of the self, for the way in which the inner self views the peripheries of the outer world determines what aspects of that world are to be made known. The self determines what it finds of immediate value or of passing interest for its operation in the outer bounds of human existence.

The self, the intangible factor which ordains man's individuality, must often move in an alien world. To live in this strange and perplexing environment, there must be knowledge of how to act, ascertain if one is right or wrong, assess the merits of a given experience, and then extract from this event a mode of behavior. This knowledge is gained, stored, evaluated, and executed by the judgment.

That the notion of judgment is one of the most important keys to an understanding of the whole of Montaigne's work may be seen by the number of times (212) that Montaigne refers to this faculty.[3] It is impossible to deal with Montaigne without an acute awareness of his concern for the faculty of judgment, whether it be with regard to himself, Montaigne the man, or to that extension of himself, Montaigne the author of the *Essais*.

Few critics have discussed Montaigne without referring to the concept of judgment which pervades his work. However, as has already been noted, many critics tend to oversimplify the semantic problem. Certainly, it would be impractical to give an account of all that has been said,

[1] No attempt will be made to differentiate between the term *jugement* and its concept. We assume for purposes of this study that, as Georges Matoré says, "le mot est lié au concept d'une manière quasi indissoluble." *La Méthode en lexicologie* (Paris, 1953), p. 33.

[2] Montaigne, *Œuvres complètes*, ed. Albert Thibaudet and Maurice Rat (Paris, 1962), I, 50, 289, i.e., Book I, Essay 50, p. 289. The stratum indicators denoting (A), (B), and (C) material have been corrected where necessary, and, unless otherwise indicated, all references are to this edition. The expression "stratum indicator" and its alphabetical representation (A, B, or C) refers to material of specific periods of composition; (A) indicates material written by Montaigne in time to appear in the 1580 edition of the *Essais*; it also includes the revisions of the 1582 and 1587 editions of Books I and II; (B) introduces material first published in 1588, and (C) material written after 1588. Throughout this study, reference to Montaigne's "suppression" of a psychological term implies that the word has been omitted through subsequent revision.

[3] For a compendium of passages which deal with the general idea of judging, see Eva Marcu, *Répertoire des idées de Montaigne* (Geneva, 1965), pp. 697–720.

within the vast corpus of Montaigne criticism, about the faculty of judgment. At best, one can select only the most pertinent studies, those studies that treat extensively, if not exclusively and specifically, the faculty of judgment.

Gabriel Compayré is particularly interested in Montaigne's ideas on education, and since, for Montaigne, education means the training of the judgment, Compayré elucidates what is meant by judging: "To judge is first of all to think for one's self. . . . To judge is to think rightly. . . . To judge well, lastly, is to be able and ready to act well." [1] Accordingly, the proper performance of these three acts is the result and goal of judgment, a faculty whose role is both intellectual and moral. As man's critical spirit, it "observes, reasons, and concludes." [2] Judgment also discerns good from evil and thus acts as our moral conscience: "It is that we may become better men that he [Montaigne] would have us better able to judge. He constantly associates those two points of view." [3] P. Mansell Jones is of the same opinion. Critical judgment and moral judgment or moral conscience are inextricably intertwined: "Judgment must be given the widest grounds for exercise, from the most trivial daily acts to the finer matters of taste; but of supreme importance is its application to moral issues, ranging from the recognition of the highest good down to the estimate of a common custom, a particular habit or an individual mode of conduct." [4]

Van den Bruwaene is particularly aware of the "nuances dans les termes qui désignent une activité de l'esprit humain." [5] He finds that one readily notices that *jugement*, *entendement*, and *intelligence* are less pejorative than *discours* and *raison*. Nevertheless, Van den Bruwaene concludes that "on ne peut considérer l'emploi de ces mots que comme une simple préférence." [6] As far as judgment is concerned, "qu'on entende par là une opération de l'esprit, un habitus ou la faculté elle-même, la raison, l'intelligence," [7] Montaigne usually looks upon it favorably. Its principal role seems to be its opposition to the excesses of reason.

1 Gabriel Compayré, *Montaigne and Education of the Judgment*, trans. J.-E. Mansion (New York, 1908), p. 66. Only the English translation of this work was available to me.

2 Compayré, pp. 68–69.

3 *Ibid.*

4 P. Mansell Jones, *French Introspectives from Montaigne to André Gide* (Cambridge, 1937), p. 36.

5 Léon Van den Bruwaene, "Les Idées philosophiques de Montaigne," *Revue néo-scolastique de philosophie*, XXXV (1933), 493.

6 Van den Bruwaene, p. 506, n. 49.

7 *Ibid.*, p. 507.

For Georges Poulet, judgment is the faculty which solidifies and immobilizes ever-changing time: "L'opération par laquelle on fait siennes les heures et les choses, n'est rien autre que le jugement." [1] In this way, judgment creates being, a being which is observable and with which one can communicate. Without judgment, the self, in its mobile fluidity, could never achieve unity. Montaigne was acutely aware of this: "Je ne peints pas l'estre. Je peints le passage: non un passage d'aage en autre, ou, comme dict le peuple, de sept en sept ans, mais de jour en jour, de minute en minute" (III, 2, 782). The journey from *passage* to *estre* is effected by means of the judgment. Thus, judgment is both an act and a faculty: "le judgement est tout entier dans une actualité.... Mais d'un autre côté il apparaît aussi comme virtualité pure. Il n'est pas ce qui est possédé, mais ce qui possède, ce qui, en fin de compte, *peut* posséder." [2]

Donald Frame presents the best available schema of the relationship of the faculties of the soul. Judgment is generally superior to common sense, although Montaigne sometimes equates them. Moreover, judgment is synonymous with reason "in the sense of *right reason* but contrasts with reason's other sense, *wrong reasoning*, by being close to the facts, patient, always ready to learn, cautious in reaching conclusions." [3] Conscience is probably one of judgment's functions; the soul is at rest when judgment is in command.[4] Of the utmost importance is its interdependency with self-study.[5]

In summary, the existing scholarship on judgment in Montaigne emphasizes two important facets of the concept: its relationship with the other faculties of the soul and its *self*-creative function. The purpose of this study is to pursue and explore in greater detail these two directions and to bring together the history or dossier of judgment, as it is found in the *Essais*. This study attempts to elucidate the meaning and the importance of the faculty of judgment in the *Essais*, its strengths, its weaknesses, its functions and activities.

Did Montaigne find the origin of the concept of judgment within himself and by himself? What was the meaning of *jugement* in the sixteenth century? Did Montaigne deal with ancient or contemporary

[1] Georges Poulet, *Etudes sur le temps humain* (Paris, 1950), p. 13.

[2] Poulet, p. 14.

[3] Donald M. Frame, *Montaigne's Discovery of Man: The Humanization of a Humanist* (New York, 1955), p. 80; see also his *Montaigne: A Biography* (New York, 1965), p. 259.

[4] Frame, *Montaigne's Discovery of Man*, p. 144.

[5] *Ibid.*, p. 80.

sources that might have influenced him in his formulation of the concept? These and other questions need to be answered in order to determine how germane and original the theme of judgment is to Montaigne's thinking and how the connotations which he attributes to this intellectual term differ, if at all, from those of his sources and of the language of the period.

In general, most dictionaries of medieval, sixteenth, and seventeenth-century French agree in their definition of judgment. Godefroy defines judgment as the "faculté de juger, de discerner, d'apprécier." Hatzfeld states that to judge is the ability to "discerner le vrai du faux"; yet he makes no mention of the faculty of judgment. Huguet is singularly remiss in that he includes neither *jugement* nor *entendement* in his compilation. [1]

Robert Estienne [2] lists *Arbitrium, Opinio, Interpretatio,* and *Judicium* as Latin equivalents of French *Jugement.* Nicot, because of his close adherence to Estienne's original, presents the very same Latin words.[3] However, as one of his examples, he offers the following formula. "Ce jugement & raison dont tous les hommes ont participation, *Sensus communis.*" With the exception of *judicium,* the Latin words all refer to an act, not to a faculty. This is also true of the Greek language, which "more often indicates an act than a faculty." [4]

Some examples of sixteenth-century usage are found in the following quotations. Frequently, the term *jugement* is used to imply a demonstration of taste, of an ability to present good and "reasonably" selected material, of a certain astuteness in measuring the worth of something which is not readily nor vigorously demonstrable. Dominique Baudier, for example, in his appraisal of the criticism directed at Montaigne, remarks that "certains, dans leurs éloges, portent aux nues son talent, son style, son jugement; d'autres le ravalent à terre." [5] La Croix du Maine, in his *Les Bibliothéques françoises* (1584), praises Montaigne, saying that "les Œuvres qu'il a mis en lumière, sont tellement suffisantes pour témoigner de sa grande doctrine & jugement

[1] Frédéric Godefroy, *Dictionnaire de l'ancienne langue française* (Paris, 1937–1938), X, 52; Adolphe Hatzfeld and Arsène Darmesteter, *Dictionnaire général de la langue française du commencement du XVIIe siècle jusqu'à nos jours* (Paris, 1926), II, 1359; Edmond Huguet, *Dictionnaire de la langue française du seizième siècle* (Paris, 1925 to date, in progress).

[2] Robert Estienne, *Les Mots françois selon l'ordre des lettres, ainsi qu'il les faut escrire, tournez en latin* (Paris, 1572).

[3] Jean Nicot, *Thresor de la langve françoise tant ancienne que Moderne* (Douceur, 1606). Reproduced from the 1621 edition by Picard et Cie, Paris, 1960.

[4] George S. Brett, *Psychology, Ancient and Modern* (New York, 1928), p. 31.

[5] Quoted in Pierre Villey, *Montaigne devant la postérité* Paris, 1935), p. 57.

émerveillable ... qu'il n'est besoin en ceci d'en parler plus avant." [1]

In other cases, judgment is considered as a faculty, but far less frequently, it seems, than as an act or a quality. As a faculty, it can connote the ability or capacity to discern one thing from another and, more particularly, the worth of that which is being measured. Du Bellay, describing his uncle's secretary, Nicolas Le Breton, observes that "il a bon jugement & sçait fort bien eslire / Le blanc d'avec le noir." [2] One is reminded of Montaigne's admonition to the prospective teacher with regard to his charge: "Qu'il luy face tout passer par l'estamine" (I, 26, 150), the *estamine* or sifter being, as it were, the image of judgment. Thus, judgment sifts that which it encompasses and then assigns to it a certain grade or worth. In addition, judgment is that faculty which enables man to ascertain the true measure of things:

> Ainsi le monde feint ne te peut nullement
> De ses appas pipeurs retenir en servage,
> S'il ne t'esteint premier d'un tenebreus nuage
> D'ignorance et d'erreur les yeus du Jugement.[3]

It remains for Montaigne to fashion a personality for judgment, to make a life-like character of it and to write its history or biography. Prior to Montaigne, the faculty of judgment was not associated with the subject of self-study. But then again, the subject of self-study is new with Montaigne: "C'est le seul livre au monde de son espece" (II, 8, 364).

The subject of sources is a difficult one. No doubt, Montaigne and La Boétie spoke often of judgment; surely it would have entailed the type of conversation that fascinated both of them. Yet, there is no trace of an explicit concern for the faculty of judgment in La Boétie's work, although the *Contr'un* or *Discours de la servitude volontaire* vociferously proclaims the right of the individual to use and to listen to his own judgment. An ardent appeal for the use of individual judgment, this work is addressed to

> ceus là qui, aians l'entendement net & l'esprit clairuoiant, ne se contentent pas, comme le gros populas, de regarder ce qui est devant leurs peids s'ils n'advisent & derriere & devant & ne rememorent ancore les choses passees pour iuger de celles du temps advenir & pour mesurer les presentes; ce sont ceus qui, aians la teste d'eus mesmes bien faite, l'ont ancore polie par l'estude & le sçavoir.[4]

[1] La Croix du Maine, *Les Bibliothèques françoises* (Paris, 1772), II, 130.

[2] Joachim Du Bellay, *Les Regrets* (Paris, 1955), p. 58.

[3] Jean-Baptiste Chassignet, *Le Mespris de la vie et consolation contre la mort* in *Poètes du XVIe siècle*, ed. Albert-Marie Schmidt (Paris, 1953), p. 948.

[4] La Boétie, *Œuvres complètes*, ed. Paul Bonnefon (Bordeaux, 1892), p. 30.

This is a capsule version of Montaigne's entire program for the meritorious conduct of life. While the suggestion of a more specifically recognizable influence or affinity of ideas with regard to the concept of judgment would be spurious, one cannot read La Boétie without being struck by the undercurrent of self-reliance and of emphasis on judgment which permeates his work. Montaigne knew him too well and shared too much in the germination and formulation of his thought not to have become imbued with it. As Frank P. Bowman has aptly remarked: "Montaigne was not a transcendent ahistorical thinker; he owed much to the books he read and the people with whom he conversed." [1]

Montaigne's translation of Raymond Sebond's *Liber creaturarum* was published in 1569. His first-hand acquaintance with this theological treatise forms the basis of his own famous essay, the "Apologie de Raimond Sebond." Just what traces of the *Liber creaturarum* remain in the *Essais* is still open to debate. Strowski speaks of "la leçon de Raymond Sebond" [2] which Montaigne learned as an adept pupil. Coppin, in his book devoted to the study of Montaigne as translator of the *Liber creaturarum*, states: "Nous voyons bien quel service Sebon a rendu à Montaigne, comment il l'a préparé à moraliser et à juger." [3] Frame, on the subject of Montaigne and religion in the "Apologie," demonstrates how aware Montaigne is of Sebond's weakness and finds that Montaigne "takes surprisingly little from Sebond." [4] At all events, what there is of Sebond in the *Essais* is found especially in the 1580 edition.[5]

Did Sebond influence Montaigne on the subject of judgment? Strowski and Coppin thought that he did, and, it seems, correctly so.

Sebond argues that his work contains the "doctrine de l'homme, et à luy propre en-tant qu'il est homme, doctrine convenable, naturelle et utile à tout homme, par laquelle il est illuminé à se cognoistre soy-mesme, son createur et presque tout ce, à quoy il est tenu comme homme." [6] But first, man must know himself; if he looks at the world about him, he will soon realize that, although he shares in many things with the other creatures of this world, he is superior to all he surveys

[1] Frank P. Bowman, *Montaigne: Essays* (London, 1965) p. 7.

[2] Fortunat Strowski, *Montaigne* (Paris, 1906), p. 81.

[3] Joseph Coppin, *Montaigne, traducteur de Raymond Sebon* (Lille, 1925), p. 117.

[4] Donald M. Frame, "Did Montaigne Betray Sebond?," *Romanic Review*, XXXVIII (1947), 316.

[5] Pierre Villey, *Les Sources et l'évolution des Essais de Montaigne* (Paris, 1908), I, 213.

[6] Sebond in *Œuvres complètes de Michel de Montaigne*, ed. Arthur Armaingaud (Paris, 1924–1941), IX, v. Montaigne's French translation of Sebond's work rather than the original Latin is quoted in this study because the latter text was not available to me.

because "le seul homme oeuvre en toute liberté. Aussi est-ce le liberal arbitre qui nous separe des autres choses: et à cause de luy dit-on que l'homme se sied au dessus de toutes les creatures." [1] At times, it is the "entendement et le liberal arbitre" [2] that differentiate man from inferior things. According to Strowski, Sebond "confond l'entendre et le libre-arbitre." [3] It may be that judgment is a part of that confusion and that by *entendement* or *libéral arbitre* Sebond implies nothing other than the critical faculty, that is judgment.

Man must avail himself of this faculty for his own well-being. One of judgment's major operations is to "affermer ou nier, croire, ou mescroire." [4] Sebond incites one to reflect personally. He looks upon his method as a *regle* which man must practice assiduously: "Pour nous exercer mieux en l'usage de nostre regle, practiquon là encore en quelques exemples." [5] Sebond considers judgment to be man's greatest privilege. Like Montaigne, Sebond demands its constant exercise; judgment is to be perfected, sharpened, and made more incisive through action, exercise, *essai*. The verb *limer* dots Montaigne's work; judgment is filed and polished in the school of experience. As Coppin states, "Montaigne a sûrement remarqué ces appels à la réflexion personnelle."[6]

Lastly, both Sebond and Montaigne think in terms of a hierarchy among the faculties of the soul. Sebond observes that "nostre ame ainsi equipee de divers offices et puissances dresse en soy comme une royauté, en laquelle ses superieures vertus commandent aux inferieures, les regissent et les gouvernent." [7] For Sebond, man's soul is not unlike a "police royale." [8] Montaigne's legalistic and hierarchical sense is no less acute. Of all his faculties, judgment occupies "un siege magistral" and it has its own private "court" where it may judge itself.[9]

Seneca's influence upon Montaigne's development is well attested. Villey has shown just how much Montaigne borrowed from Seneca's *Epistles*, especially prior to 1580 and after 1588.[10] Montaigne gleans many things in his reading of Seneca; critics stress Montaigne's so-called "stoical period," perhaps best exemplified in Montaigne by the

[1] Sebond, p. 102.
[2] *Ibid.*, p. 114.
[3] Strowski, p. 78.
[4] Sebond, p. 116.
[5] *Ibid.*, p. 120.
[6] Coppin, p. 105.
[7] Sebond, p. 179.
[8] *Ibid.*, p. 183.
[9] III, 13, 1052; III, 2, 785.
[10] Villey, I, 215. Between 1580 and 1588, Montaigne seems to have obtained only 12 statements from his reading of the *Epistles*.

theme of death. However, few have acknowledged the existence of certain very definite and simular ideas on the subject of judgment to be found in both Seneca and Montaigne.[1]

Seneca deals harshly with man's judgment. On the whole, he feels that it is a feeble, uncertain, and imperfect instrument, treacherous, unknowing of its own ways, incapable of constancy: "Variatur cotidie iudicium et in contrarium vertitur ac plerisque agitur vita per lusum." [2] Montaigne, in one of many examples, follows suit in his discussion of tastes in dress and ever-changing styles. Indeed, our judgment is so subject to change that even all the tailors in the world would be unable to invent enough styles to satisfy it. For lack of invention, the old replaces the new, and it is not unusual "qu'un mesme jugement preigne, en l'espace de quinze ou vingt ans, deux ou trois, non diverses seulement, mais contraires opinions, d'une inconstance et legereté incroyable" (I, 49, 285). Montaigne wrote an entire essay on "De l'inconstance de nos actions." In it, he follows the Senecan original closely: "Ce que nous avons à cett' heure proposé, nous le changeons tantost, et tantost encore retournons sur nos pas; ce n'est que branle et inconstance" (II, 1, 316).

Man's judgment is a prey to disease, and disease is none other than "iudicium in pravo pertinax, tamquam valde expetenda sint, quae leviter expetenda sunt." [3] On the chapter of the subjection of the judgment to the passions, Montaigne is inexhaustible. The terms *maladie, imbécillité, faiblesse, renverser, ébranler, tourneboułer*, constantly appear in his discussions of judgment. Unwarranted lust for glory and reputation, as well as stupid recollection and regurgitation of knowledge, are the symptoms of a diseased judgment. How much better it would be if man accepted the approval of his own judgment, if man could learn to rely upon his own evaluation of himself, his personal strengths and capabilities! Montaigne echoes Seneca's urge to self-reliance: "Mais nous, que disons nous nous mesmes? que jugeons nous? que faisons-nous?" (I, 25, 136).[4]

[1] The only notable exception is Camilla Hill Hay, who, in her *Montaigne, lecteur et imitateur de Sénèque* (Poitiers, 1938), states that many of Montaigne's ideas repeat what is a constant theme in Seneca, i.e., "la faiblesse et l'incertitude de notre jugement," p. 133.

[2] Seneca, *Ad Lucilium Epistulae Morales*, trans. Richard M. Gummere, The Loeb Classical Library (London, 1925), I, 136–137: "Judgment varies from day to day, and changes to the opposite, making many a man pass his life in a kind of game."

[3] Seneca, II, 142–143: "a persistent perversion of the judgment, so that things which are mildly desirable are thought to be highly desirable."

[4] Seneca, I, 238–239: "'Hoc Zenon dixit'; tu quid? 'Hoc Cleanthes'; tu quid?" "'This is what Zeno said.' But what have you yourself said? 'This is the opinion of Cleanthes.' But what is your own opinion?"

While Seneca may have berated judgment unmercifully, Montaigne found in Seneca that self-reliance is both an attribute and one of the functions of judgment. For Seneca, the supreme good was virtue, and virtue was "iudicium verum et inmotum." [1]

Montaigne's affection and esteem for Plutarch never wavered, never changed. Throughout the whole of his work, Montaigne has included 398 direct borrowings from or allusions to the work of Plutarch.[2] Montaigne often draws contrasts between Plutarch and Seneca, and the advantage is generally given to the former because Montaigne prefers the depth, the soundness, and the enduring warmth and humanity of Plutarch's thought.[3] Plutarch does not discuss or present a theory of the concept of judgment. Rather, it may be said that he lives it, that his entire work is the act and symbol of judgment, and that Montaigne learned from him what the purpose of judgment was and what its productions could or should be: "Le véritable éducateur du jugement de Montaigne, c'est Plutarque." [4]

Plutarch, whether it be in the *Moralia* or in the *Lives*, always reflects upon the examples which he advances; he passes judgment or he judges; in fact, he moralizes. Unlike Sextus Empiricus, who, in his *Hypotyposes*, compiles example upon example, building a veritable arsenal of intellectual weaponry, but without commenting on its merits, Plutarch demonstrates the application of judgment to moral issues. He not only recognizes the existence of fact, but also attempts to analyze, interpret, and judge that which he observes. What he observes most, what he deems most worthy of the operation of judgment, is man: "Le premier service que rend Plutarque à Montaigne, c'est de l'habituer à s'observer soi-même de près, et à observer les autres autour de lui." [5]

It is Plutarch who may have set the course by which Montaigne arrived at the interconnection and interdependency of judgment and discovery of the self. Plutarch's depictions of life could only sharpen Montaigne's awareness of the complexity of the self and of the desirability of fathoming it with what seemed the most appropriate instrument, the faculty of judgment.

[1] Seneca, II, 92-93: "A true and never-swerving judgment."

[2] Villey, I, 200.

[3] III, 12, 1017: "La façon de Plutarque, d'autant qu'elle est plus desdaigneuse et plus destendue, elle est, selon moy, d'autant plus virile et persuasive; je croyrois ayséement que son ame avoit les mouvements plus asseurez et plus reiglés. L'un, plus vif, nous pique et eslance en sursaut, touche plus l'esprit. L'autre, plus rassis, nous informe, establit et conforte constamment, touche plus l'entendement. Celuy là ravit nostre jugement, cestuy-cy le gaigne."

[4] Villey, II, 106.

Pierre Villey, *Les Essais de Montaigne* (Paris, 1946), p. 55.

Montaigne's early appraisal of Cicero is well known: "Si j'ai employé une heure à le lire, qui est beaucoup pour moy, et que je r'amentoive ce que j'en ay tiré de suc et de substance, la plus part du temps je n'y treuve que du vent" (II, 10, 393). Cicero's periodic style repelled Montaigne. He sought to become wiser, and Cicero showed him only "ces ordonnances logiciennes et Aristoteliques" (II, 10, 393). It was not until after 1588 that Montaigne's attitude toward Cicero became a more favorable one. Cicero's moral treatises now form part of Montaigne's regular reading. The two works of Cicero which he seems to prefer are the *Tusculan Disputations* and the *Academics*.

What Montaigne incorporates into his own text varies a great deal, but the one Ciceronian theme which recurs most often is that of the freedom of the judgment to rely on itself, and itself alone, in its search for truth, whether it be the inner truth of the self or the outer truth of the world which surrounds it. In "Du repentir," Montaigne admits that he judges himself according to his own standards, for only he is capable of going beyond conjecture in his appraisal of himself. Others, "vous devinent par conjectures incertaines; ils voyent non tant vostre nature que vostre art. Par ainsi ne vous tenez pas à leur sentence; tenez vous à la vostre" (III, 2, 785). Later, he adds: "Tuo tibi judicio est utendum." [1] Throughout the (C) additions, Montaigne reinforces his faith in the ability of the individual judgment to raise man above himself.

The Pyrrhonists advocated the suspension of judgment, the immobility of the critical faculty; they wanted it made powerless, capable of intellectual search but not of decision. On the contrary, Cicero stresses the freedom of judgment, its ennobling qualities, and the marked individuality with which it surrounded its user, Montaigne's "homme d'entendement":

Sapientis est enim proprium nihil quod poenitere possit facere, nihil invitum, splendide, constanter, graviter, honeste omnia, nihil ita exspectare quasi certo futurum, nihil cum acciderit admirari, ut inopinatum ac novum accidisse videatur, omnia ad suum arbitrium referre, suis stare iudiciis; quo quid sit beatius mihi certe in mentem venire non potest.[2]

[1] Cicero, *Tusculan Disputations*, trans. J. E. King, The Loeb Classical Library (London, 1927), pp. 218–219: "you must use your own judgment."

[2] Cicero, pp. 508–509: "For it is characteristic of the wise man to do nothing of which he can repent, nothing against his will, to do everything nobly, consistently, soberly, rightly, not to look forward to anything as if it were bound to come, to be astonished at no occurrence under the impression that its occurrence is unexpected and strange, to bring all things to the standard of his own judgment, to abide by his own decisions. And what can be happier than this I certainly cannot conceive."

One finds in Cicero the same sense of pride in and high regard for his own faculties that one readily associates with Montaigne. The latter considers judgment his prime faculty and is wont to express his faith in its ability to remain free, unpreoccupied, individualistic, and personal; in sum, as represented by its acts, it is the intellectual representation of the man himself. No doubt, in his late years, Montaigne enjoyed Cicero more and more every day because he came to admire Cicero's highly personal stance vis-à-vis his belief in his own judgment:

defendat quod quisque sentit; sunt enim iudicia libera: nos institutum tenebimus nulliusque unius disciplinae legibus astricte, quibus in philosophia necessario pareamus, quid sit in quaque re maxime probabile semper requiremus; quod cum saepe alias tum nuper in Tusculano studiose egimus.[1]

The subject of sources and influence has been avowedly more suggestive than conclusive. Source studies are not a simple matter, and the demarcation line between influence and affinity is a thin and often invisible one. As Villey said, in his discussion of Plutarch and matters of morals, "la communauté d'idées, en pareille matière, n'indique pas toujours une influence." [2] However, affinities, if not sources, can be relevant, especially when dealing with Montaigne, and should be pointed out, particularly when general relationships have already been established.

Montaigne's notion of judgment did not change abruptly from one point of view to another. Rather, it evolved gradually, as Montaigne became better acquainted with the purpose of his *Essais*. The concept of judgment discussed in this study is fundamentally Montaigne's; as far as can be ascertained, no tract, of any kind, on psychology, existed which could have provided him with the semantic and ideational possibilities which he attributes to the faculty of judgment in the *Essais*. Montaigne's notion of judgment took on new and added life in his readings of Sebond, Seneca, Plutarch, and Cicero, but the inner and permanent core of judgment was the product of Montaigne's observation of his period of history and of himself.

[1] *Ibid.*, pp. 334–335: "let everyone defend his views, for judgment is free: I shall cling to my rule and without being tied to the laws of any single school of thought which I feel bound to obey, shall always search for the most probable solution in every problem; and as had been my frequent practice on other occasions, so I was careful to act lately in my house at Tusculum."

[2] Pierre Villey, *Les Livres d'histoire moderne utilisés par Montaigne* (Paris, 1908), p. 211.

CHAPTER I

IGNORANCE, FORMATION, AND OPERATION

Montaigne's use of the term *jugement* does not lend itself to easy analysis. The modern temperament does not find the word unusual, striking, or complex and is apt to dismiss too readily the intricacies which it includes for Montaigne. Furthermore, there is no simple way of presenting exactly what Montaigne means by judgment. Frequently, the context itself is not sufficient to elucidate the meaning. One must rely on one's familiarity with the other uses of the term throughout Montaigne's work. Moreover, the concept of judgment is so woven into the fabric of the *Essais* that a discussion of judgment often entails a fairly detailed setting.

In 1563, after La Boétie's death, Montaigne wrote to his father "concernant quelques particularitez qu'il remarqua en la maladie & mort de feu monsieur de La Boétie." [1] This mournful and touching letter contains the earliest example of the term *jugement* in Montaigne's known writings. Montaigne describes La Boétie's last moments. Having taken leave of his wife, La Boétie asked Montaigne to remain at his side. As death approached, La Boétie's voice became louder and more penetrating; he began to twist and turn violently in his bed. At one point, he asked Montaigne to make room for him:

> Lors entre autres choses il se print à me prier & reprier avecques une extreme affection, de luy donner une place: de sorte que j'eus peur que son jugement fust esbranlé.[2]

Montaigne's fear that his good friend might have lost his judgment is

[1] "Fragment d'une lettre," *Œuvres complètes*, ed. Albert Thibaudet and Maurice Rat (Paris, 1962), p. 1347. Although this letter was not published until 1570, it is likely that it was written shortly after the death of La Boétie.

[2] *Ibid.*, p. 1359.

not unfounded; La Boétie's condition could indicate little else. But is it La Boétie's judgment which is unsettled, impaired, unstrung? Is not La Boétie's appeal to Montaigne "de luy donner une place" an indication that La Boétie has momentarily lost his senses, that he is in the throes of a hallucinatory experience? Montaigne implies quite literally that La Boétie has lost touch with reality. The faculty of judgment evoked in this passage is not the same judgment whose formation and education Montaigne advocates in "De l'institution des enfans." Judgment here is more visceral. Without yet delving into the details of the *jugement-entendement* relationship, one would probably accept, given the same situation, Etienne Pasquier's terminology, when he, in turn, described Montaigne's final hours: "il demeura trois jours entiers, plein d'entendement, sans pouvoir parler." [1] Perhaps Montaigne is referring to La Boétie's inability to "discerner le vrai du faux"; [2] however, La Boétie's faculty of judgment, as it is presented in this passage, is more organic than that. Judgment is a complex faculty, and it has many connotations and many attributes.

Montaigne was always concerned with the notion of judging and of what or whom should be judged: "Certes, c'est un subject merveilleusement vain, divers et ondoyant, que l'homme. Il est malaisé d'y fonder jugement constant et uniforme" (I, 1, 13). Written in 1578–1580,[3] these lines emphasize what has already become Montaigne's primary occupation, the analysis and evaluation of man, and more particularly of man as he sees him within himself:

> Je propose une vie basse et sans lustre, c'est tout un. On attache aussi bien toute la philosophie morale à une vie populaire et privée que à une vie de plus riche estoffe; chaque homme porte la forme entière de l'humaine condition (III, 2, 782)

Undoubtedly, Montaigne's curiosity and inquisitiveness know no bounds. He is fascinated by all psychic and moral phenomena and driven by the desire to express his opinion, whatever the subject. For Montaigne, personal reaction is in the nature of things; observation and recording alone do not suffice.

Experience has shown Montaigne that judgment must be acquired, fashioned, and utilized according to a pattern. As a moralist, he endeavors to impart his knowledge concerning the acquisition of judgment. The result of this desire is "De l'institution des enfans," a significant

[1] "Lettre à M. de Pelgé," *Les Œuvres* (Amsterdam, 1723), II, 518.
[2] Hatzfeld and Darmesteter, II, 1359.
[3] All dates pertaining to the *Essais* follow the chronology established by Pierre Villey.

essay because "une pédagogie implique une philosophie de la vie." [1] It so happens that the term *jugement*, better than any other, demonstrates Montaigne's philosophy of life. In great part, the concept of judgment functions as an extension of his own mind; the characteristics of judgment, what it is and what it should be, are found in Montaigne's own patterns of thought. In other words, how Montaigne himself thinks determines many of the attributes, and more importantly, the operation of judgment as he sees it. "De l'institution des enfans" is not only a pedagogical program; it is also Montaigne's own personal creation, the system by which he has developed and strengthened his own "jugement naturel."

IGNORANCE AND JUDGMENT

Montaigne is unflagging in his juxtaposition of judgment and memory, and he never leaves one in doubt as to where he stands. Although he despises the pedant and all things artificial in general, he particularly dislikes the self-satisfied demonstration of memory:

> Qui regardera de bien près à ce genre de gens, qui s'estend bien loing, il trouvera, comme moy, que le plus souvent ils ne s'entendent, ny autruy, et qu'ils ont la souvenance assez pleine, mais le jugement entierement creux, sinon que leur nature d'elle mesme le leur ait autrement façonné (I, 25, 138).

Memory is a storehouse whose inventory is of little value if unaccompanied by judgment. The word "creux" implies that judgment is also a container of sorts; however, the verb "façonner" marks the major difference. Judgment is an active faculty which is fashioned by exercise, whereas memory, which is passive in nature, can only receive and retain.

With few exceptions, Montaigne refers pejoratively to memory. He constantly associates it with knowledge or *science*: "C'est le receptacle et l'estuy de la science que la memoire" (II, 17, 634). *Science* normally denotes a lack of felicitous knowledge or a knowledge misbegotten and misapplied: "C'est par l'entremise de nostre ignorance plus que de nostre science que nous sommes sçavans de ce divin sçavoir" (II, 12, 480). *Mémoire* and *science* hinder judgment in its operation and, all too often, are considered as a manifestation of judgment: "si en mon païs on veut dire qu'un homme n'a poinct de sens, ils disent qu'il n'a point de memoire" (I, 9, 35).

Science is an appendage, a cumbersome piece of baggage that

[1] Villey, *Les Essais de Montaigne*, p. 88.

needlessly and nefariously impedes the orderly progress of judgment. Knowledge must be organic, a second nature, as it were: "il ne faut pas attacher le sçavoir à l'ame, il l'y faut incorporer; il ne l'en faut pas arrouser, il l'en faut teindre" (I, 25, 139). Memory is a shell, an envelope, a façade; it reacts to knowledge, to experience, as does a tablet of wax to a knife; a record is made, an imprint is left, but neither the memory nor the wax is fundamentally altered. That which undergoes change, that which must change, is judgment, the faculty which not only stores experience, but also digests it: "Qu'il ne luy demande pas seulement compte des mots de sa leçon, mais du sens et de la substance" (I, 26, 149).

Judgment is the inner part of man and the most important of his faculties. Memory is an adjunct, a factitious exterior; it parrots while judgment assimilates: "Il ne dira pas tant sa leçon, comme il la fera" (I, 26, 167). As Thibaudet has remarked, "contraste entre intérieur et extérieur – contraste entre vivant et mécanique – une idée constante de Montaigne." [1]

Montaigne insists on penetrating all surface and artificial appearances. When he looks at a man, when he studies a literary work in order to find the man, not the author, behind the work, he is indulging in his favorite pastime: the search for reality. The true meaning of all beings and things lies within their palpable bounds, and knowledge depends upon the removal of the incrustations. Montaigne thinks in terms of exposing these fabricated extensions of self with which the individual and society surround themselves.

Memory accumulates trash and creates obstacles for judgment. Judgment thrives upon motion and change, and memory stands in its path by being a heavy, clumsy, and unwieldy instrument. Memory is an impediment to the study of man. In conversation, it tends to take the lead to the detriment of judgment. Montaigne has witnessed such occurrences even among his best and most private friends, and Montaigne does not choose his friends carelessly:

> à mesure que la memoire leur fournit la chose entiere et presente, ils reculent si arriere leur narration, et la chargent de vaines circonstances, que si le conte est bon, ils en estouffent la bonté; s'il ne l'est pas, vous estes à maudire ou l'heur de leur memoire, ou le malheur de leur jugement (I, 9, 35–36).

Humorously, Montaigne points out one of the activities in which memory must be engaged: "Ce n'est pas sans raison qu'on dit que qui

[1] Albert Thibaudet, *Montaigne*, ed. Floyd Gray (Paris, 1963), p. 444.

ne se sent point assez ferme de memoire, ne se doit pas mesler d'estre menteur" (I, 9, 36). Falsehood and memory need each other; such a suture not only deprecates memory, but also underlines further the exterior aspect, the "falsehood" of memory. Memory is attacked at every turn and often insidiously.

Science tends to assert its supposed superiority and authority over the proper exercise of judgment. Man regiments the search for knowledge. Experts everywhere demand to be believed, and, consequently, *science*, an imperfect and doubtful instrument at best, is called upon to aid man in his pursuit of that wisdom which should enable him to rise above his condition. As a result, judgment is rendered powerless, and man is perhaps farther from the truth than ever before:

> Le dialecticien se rapporte au grammairien de la signification des mots; le rhetoricien emprunte du dialecticien les lieux des arguments; le poëte, du musicien les mesures; le geometrien, de l'arithmeticien les proportions; les metaphysiciens prennent pour fondement les conjectures de la physique. Car chasque science a ses principes presupposez par où le jugement humain est bridé de toutes parts (II, 12, 522).

Since memory and *science* represent knowledge, judgment, their opposite, must connote the absence of knowledge or, at least, the absence of a certain kind of knowledge. Whenever Montaigne speaks of the faculty of judgment, he implies a sort of general ignorance. One of Montaigne's basic assumptions is that ignorance forms a part of judgment. Judgment cannot function propitiously unless it ignores certain facts:

> Je m'aide à perdre ce que je serre particulierement.... Je sçay en general le nom des arts et ce dequoy elles traictent, mais rien au delà. Je feuillette les livres, je ne les estudie pas: ce qui m'en demeure, c'est chose que je ne reconnois plus estre d'autruy; c'est cela seulement dequoy mon jugement a faict son profict, les discours et les imaginations dequoy il s'est imbu; l'autheur, le lieu, les mots et autres circonstances, je les oublie incontinent (II, 17, 634–635).

However, to ignore is to neglect something willfully, and ignorance, for Montaigne, is somewhat more generic and automatic. The relationship of judgment and the proper attainment of knowledge is delineated further in the contrast which he draws between the verbs *savoir* and *juger*. When one says "je sais," one speaks of information, of some sort of acquisition. There is a finality about *savoir*. *Juger*, on the other hand, deals with intangibles that are not readily verifiable. There is an openness to *juger*, an awareness of shades and grades, that is based upon the acceptance of the idea that facts are not all and that perhaps behind them there lies a truer and fuller meaning. One approaches and benefits from experience by means of ignorance, a state of mind untrammeled by dead weight, that is by memory and *science.*

By ignorance, Montaigne may mean the failure to know a specific fact. However, he more often assigns to ignorance the meaning of a permanent condition of the judgment in which things are neither fixed nor dogmatic. In a certain sense, judgment is or should be a blank. It should approach matters as a free agent, as an agent whose capabilities are not hampered by personal interest, prejudices, passions, or *science.* Judgment does not exist in and of itself, as do many of the other faculties. Judgment brings itself into being, creates itself, by utilizing what natural gifts it finds at hand and by anchoring itself in experience. Judgment exists by means of its interaction with phenomena, and it must be able to analyze and interpret lucidly what it encounters. Because it is such a vital faculty for the development and moral progress of the individual, judgment must act from the position of strength which only ignorance can afford it.

Judgment is born of ignorance; ignorance, or *inscience* as Poulet calls it,[1] is the pedestal of judgment. The effective operation of judgment depends upon the interaction of ignorance and experience; ignorance engenders the desire of inquiry while experience controls the event and makes it its own.

Montaigne undertakes the *essai* of life and of himself, secure in the knowledge that judgment will bear fruit, see him through, and enable him to continue his tests or trials. In Montaigne's mind, the primary faculty is judgment; if this faculty did not also imply ignorance, perhaps *s'essayer* would not be as important to him as *se réaliser.* One of judgment's primary functions is to perpetuate the *essai,* and it can do so only through a willingness on the part of man to submit himself to its scrutiny. Judgment can function only if true knowledge is its object, for the pursuit of knowledge fosters the withdrawal of ignorance.

Judgment seeks knowledge, but the former is by far the more important of the two:

La science et la verité peuvent loger chez nous sans jugement, et le jugement y peut aussi estre sans elles (II, 10, 388).

et encore que ces deux pieces soyent necessaires et qu'il faille qu'elles s'y trouvent toutes deux, si est-ce qu'à la verité celle du sçavoir est moins prisable que celle du jugement (I, 25, 139).

Even when Montaigne is somewhat conciliatory where "science" is

[1] Poulet, p. 13.

concerned, an ingrained dislike of "science" is evident in his choice of words: *loger* contrasts with *estre*. Nevertheless, "c'est une bonne drogue que la science; mais nulle drogue n'est assez forte pour se preserver sans alteration et corruption, selon le vice du vase qui l'estuye" (I, 25, 140). "Science" can be good only if it is so incorporated and assimilated by the judgment that it is no longer recognizable as a separate entity. Otherwise, judgment is considerably better off when left to its own devices.

Few people seem to be able to combine successfully judgment and knowledge, as the phrase "les personnes rares et excellentes en jugement et en sçavoir" (I, 25, 132) indicates. In fact, Montaigne thinks that only one person has consistently demonstrated to a high degree the effective amalgamation of both: Plutarch, "qui est de tous les autheurs que je cognoisse celuy qui a mieux meslé l'art à la nature et le jugement à la science" (III, 6, 876). No doubt, *art* and particularly *nature* are problematic words when wielded by Montaigne.[1] *Nature* has many acceptations; however, since Montaigne is saying in effect that *science* is to *art* as *jugement* is to *nature*, one can see in these parallels the continuation of the exterior-interior theme. *Art* and *science* cover and hide, usually unfortunately, seldom happily, the inner being, both *nature* and *jugement*. Ignorance, an important part of judgment, is intimately connected to *nature*, *naturel*; that which is *ignorant* and *naturel* is simple, ingenuous, unsophisticated, naïve. Hence, because of its ignorance, judgment resembles nature; both are spontaneous, instinctive, and flexible. Montaigne often refers to judgment as "naturel" because judgment is a most precious faculty and "naturel" implies approval: "Quant aux facultez naturelles qui sont en moy, dequoy c'est icy l'essay, je les sens flechir sous la charge. Mes conceptions et mon jugement ne marche qu'à tastons" (I, 26, 145). "Naturel" is that which is best and of the highest good for the individual.[2] Ignorance, in the positive sense of the term, like nature, is man's watchdog, which points out to him the contours of his "humanness": "L'ignorance qui se sçait, qui se juge et qui se condamne, ce n'est pas une entiere ignorance: pour l'estre, il faut qu'elle s'ignore soy-mesme" (II, 12, 482).

Montaigne distinguishes judgment from information. The individual

[1] Neal Dow, *The Concept and Term "Nature" in Montaigne's Essays* (Philadelphia, 1940), has shown the complexities and pitfalls involved in the study of this concept. Although many critics have dealt with *nature*, sixteenth-century studies still lack an appreciation of the term *art*.

[2] Dow, p. 63, remarks that "by attaching the word 'natural' to a sensation, a phenomenon, an institution, Montaigne affixes his approval to it."

can obtain particular knowledge through "science" and memory, but the powers of discernment and general knowledge are an inherent part of man: "si l'on m'y force, je suis contraint, assez ineptement, d'en tirer quelque matiere de propos universel, sur quoy j'examine son jugement naturel" (I, 26, 144); the individual's "jugement naturel" need only be exercised for attainment of its full potential.

Memory is a receptacle of theory, whereas judgment is experience, that which has come to life, that which is still alive. For Montaigne, the material experience, not knowledge *per se*, is of the utmost importance. The faculties of the soul, and especially judgment, grow stronger and improve in proportion to the weakening of memory. Judgment, personal inventiveness, and self-reliance are deadened and stunted by memory: "[j'] irois facilement couchant et allanguissant mon esprit et mon jugement sur les traces d'autruy ... si les inventions et opinions estrangieres m'estoient presentes par le benefice de la memoire" (I, 9, 35). Judgment must be constantly on the alert. When it falters, when it slumbers, as it often does, man falls prey to the baser, irrational, emotional side of his nature, and misery inevitably ensues.

Judgment is man's power of reflection. When one reflects, surveys, judges, one is involved in the process of conception. Hence, judgment or the exercise of judgment creates ideas; these ideas, these personal creations are what Montaigne presents in the *Essais*. Montaigne seeks to penetrate, to unearth everything which comes within his purview, for knowledge is reflection:

> Le mediter est un puissant estude et plein, à qui sçait se taster et employer vigoureusement: j'aime mieux forger mon ame que la meubler. Il n'est point d'occupation ny plus foible, ny plus forte, que celle d'entretenir ses pensées selon l'ame que c'est. Les plus grandes en font leur vacation.... Aussi l'a nature favorisée de ce privilege qu'il n'y a rien que nous puissions faire si long temps, ny action à la quelle nous nous addonons plus ordinairement et facilement .... La lecture me sert specialement à esveiller par divers objects mon discours, à embesongner mon jugement, non ma memoyre (III, 3, 797).

The opposition of judgment and memory recurs throughout the *Essais*. Montaigne is proud of his faculty of judgment, and he seldom feels that he suffers from a lack of it: the phrase "ce peu de jugement que j'ay" [1] contains an unusual admission, which is readily explained by the nature of its context. On the other hand, he constantly berates memory, and he is wont to point out, whenever he can, that little or no

[1] In Montaigne's "Advertissement au lecteur" written in 1570 for the publication of La Boétie's translation of *La Mesnagerie de Xénophon*. The entire "Advertissement au lecteur" is reproduced in the Thibaudet-Rat edition, p. 1719.

memory is one of his great inadequacies: "... moy, qui, à faute de memoire ... "(II, 10, 388); "je n'ay pas ... assez de memoire"; "c'est un outil de merveilleux service que la memoire, et sans lequel le jugement faict bien à peine son office: elle me manque du tout" (II, 17, 632). Memory may not be Montaigne's strongest faculty; yet, anyone capable of riddling one's writing with the numerous Latin quotations that he seems to have been able to recall at will is far from being totally deficient.

Montaigne's work abounds in self-deprecatory statements, and, in general, they seem to be made with abandon and, more significantly, with reason. As Frank P. Bowman has pointed out, "there is something of the *poseur* about these claims of incompetency." [1] Montaigne loves paradox; in essence, by downgrading the role of memory and stressing the advantages of judgment and its mate ignorance, he is saying that one knows more by knowing less; in fact, he humiliates himself in order to enhance himself, for "il se voit par experience ... que les memoires excellentes se joignent volontiers aux jugemens debiles" (I, 9, 35).

Judgment is the faculty which Montaigne cherishes the most and which he unfailingly presents as his greatest good, his "forme sienne." However, judgment is always accompanied by ignorance, and ignorance, with its connotation of simplicity, naïveté, and particularly openness and sincerity, evokes very well Montaigne's man-centered and practical attitude towards life. In "Du jeune Caton," written in 1572–1574, Montaigne speaks of his judgment as "cette maistresse partie" (I, 37, 225). After 1588, he remarks that, when it pleases him, he can give himself to doubt and uncertainty "et à ma maistresse forme, qui est l'ignorance" (I, 50, 290). Judgment and ignorance, two sides of the same coin, cross and span the length and breadth of the *Essais*.

FORMATION OF JUDGMENT

If judgment is to be formed and trained, it must be given the greatest possible exposure. Although Montaigne is concerned with the training of judgment in the young, he is primarily interested in the improvement and demonstration of his own. Throughout the *Essais*, but particularly in Books I and II, Montaigne endeavors to sharpen his judgment. An analysis of how, why, and what he judges can shed further light on other important facets of judgment.

The essay "De Democritus et Heraclitus," (I, 50; 1572–1580), com-

[1] Bowman, p. 46.

prises, in its original structure, three distinct movements. Part one involves a presentation of the objects of judgment. Part two reveals Montaigne's purpose in the essay, and part three is a demonstration of his judgment in one of its operations.

The first part begins with the famous statement, "le jugement est un util à tous subjects, et se mesle par tout. A cette cause, aux essais que j'en fay ici, j'y employe toute sorte d'occasion" (I, 50, 289). What is of significance is the kind of subjects that Montaigne mentions. He puts his judgment to the test on subjects he does not understand at all. If, as he must soon realize, he is unable to deal competently with the subject, he withdraws, thereby acknowledging his deficiency. Such an admission is one of judgment's activities and one in which it takes great pride. At times, Montaigne likes to deal with a vain and ephemeral subject in order to see if his judgment can make something of it and support it. Thirdly, he brings his judgment face to face with a well-known and noble subject about which everything has been said. In these cases, his judgment must follow others, and its function is to decide which is the best way and which of the thousand paths that lead to the subject has been the most wisely chosen.

In part two, Montaigne remarks that any subject is suitable but adds that he normally takes the first one that comes to mind. Caesar is a good example. Whether he is directing the battle of Pharsalia or planning love affairs, one still sees his mind at work. After 1588, Montaigne adds: "Tout mouvement nous descouvre" (I, 50, 290).

Having delineated the province of judgment, Montaigne discusses the avowed subject of the essay: Democritus and Heraclitus. These two philosophers upheld two diametrically opposed views of the human condition. Democritus thought that the human condition was vain and ridiculous, and, consequently, he always wore a mocking and laughing face in public. On the contrary, Heraclitus was constantly sad and sorrowful, for he pitied the human condition. Hence, it can be seen that Montaigne is going to apply his judgment to what he considers to be the third type of subject open to the activity of judgment, that is choosing or deciding which of two or more ideas or possibilities is the right one. Montaigne unhesitatingly declares:

> j'ayme mieux la premiere humeur, non par ce qu'il est plus plaisant de rire que de pleurer, mais parce qu'elle est plus desdaigneuse, et qu'elle nous condamne plus que l'autre (I, 50, 291).

Montaigne has presented two different outlooks on how one should consider the human condition, not because he is particularly interested in what Democritus or Heraclitus have to say about it, but because their attitudes enable him to express his own personal view on the matter, that is to judge whose conclusion is the correct one. What Democritus and Heraclitus said is not important. *What Montaigne thinks* is the purpose of the essay; he has used Democritus and Heraclitus as a springboard: the trajectory, the execution of the maneuver, and the point of impact are what interest the spectator, not the point of departure:

Qu'on ne s'attende point aux choses, dequoy je parle, mais a ma façon d'en parler et à la creance que j'en ay. Ce que je desrobe d'autruy, ce n'est pas pour le faire mien, je ne pretens icy nulle part, que celle de raisonner et de juger: le demeurant n'est pas de mon rolle.

After 1588, Montaigne substituted: "Qu'on ne s'attende pas aux matieres, mais à la façon que j'y donne" (II, 10, 387).

In his early period, Montaigne's concern for the development of his judgment leads him to treat short and isolated topics upon which he can superimpose his judgment, thereby exercising and strengthening it. However, what he is also fashioning and strengthening is the projection of himself, for one depicts oneself by judging. As Caesar presents himself in love as well as in war, Montaigne declares himself in the judging of any and all topics: "Ce sont icy mes fantasies, par lesquelles je ne tasche point à donner à connoistre les choses, mais moy" (II, 10, 387). Montaigne knows that his faculty of judgment can only be measured by means of the judgments it renders and the ideas it generates. Both judgments and personal ideas will gain in depth, perception, and accuracy through the constant involvement of the faculty of judgment with life. The more he judges, the more acute his judgment will be.

To judge is to express one's personal and preferably original thoughts, whatever the subject, realizing that to judge is also to be judged. It is for this reason that the formation of judgment in the young occupies such an important part in Montaigne's thought.

The acts of a free judgment constitute one of the more important aspects of man's life. Man is the object of judgment; everything he does is open to question and demands interpretation. The man who judges is in turn judged by his fellow men, intellectually, morally, and socially; in each instance, man's faculty of judgment is propelled by the desire for self-improvement. In his discussion of the young man's "institution," Montaigne's reference to judgment seems to imply character, that is moral character. Montaigne envisages man as he is seen in his behavior in general and in his moral conduct in particular.

Negatively, man's faculty of judgment connotes ignorance, one of the inquisitive and intellectual aspects of judgment. On the other hand, judgment is more than an intellectual faculty. Judgment is the faculty which should improve the most throughout man's lifetime. Because it is entrusted with the care of man's moral improvement, it is closely associated with conscience. It is for this reason that Montaigne singles out judgment as the faculty to be trained above all others; Montaigne is concerned with man's total education, intellectual and moral. Hence, one espies the injection of a strong moral undercurrent in the concept of judgment, and one can never exclude it when discussing judgment.

Montaigne believes in man's capabilities. For him, "education can be positive. Hard as it is to force our inclinations, we can train them by habit and control them by judgment. More and more judgment is the key faculty for Montaigne, the one by which man can and should rise above mere nature." [1] Initially, Montaigne did not hold this optimistic view; he was prepared to accept baseness of nature and moral decrepitude as man's lot in life. Despite the fact that Montaigne emerges from the "Apologie de Raimond Sebond" with a renewed sense of strength within himself and within man, he never ceases to berate judgment and emphasize its shortcomings and limitations. This aspect of judgment will be treated in the next chapter, "The Limitations of Judgment."

The great diversity of opinions which one encounters in all subjects demonstrates man's ineptitude in matters of judgment. Some men are capable of assimilating the objects of judgment "en leur vray estre, mais mille autres leur donnent un estre nouveau et contraire chez eux" (I, 14, 50). Man is not impaired by a lack of the necessary mental equipment in order to measure accurately the reality of all things, for "les hommes sont tous d'une espece, et sauf le plus et le moins, se trouvent garnis de pareille outils et instrumens pour concevoir et juger" (I, 14, 50). The difficulty lies usually in the fact that man's natural abilities have not been properly channeled; man's judgment, an inherent part of his nature, has not been developed by practice, by art. In a sense, nature and art complement each other throughout the maturation of judgment.

Man's faculty of judgment is inborn and acquired. Montaigne, in

[1] Frame, *Montaigne's Discovery of Man*, p. 104.

"Des livres," claims that he is trying or testing only his natural faculties, that is his judgment, as he has stated elsewhere: [1] "C'est icy purement l'essay de mes facultez naturelles, et nullement des acquises" (II, 10, 387). When Montaigne finds that he must question a child on matters of particular knowledge, he manages to substitute "quelque matiere de propos universel, sur quoy j'examine son jugement naturel: leçon qui leur est autant incognue, comme à moy la leur" (I, 26, 144). Hence, "jugement naturel" implies an innate quality or faculty which in and of itself is able to deal, albeit primitively, with the realm of knowledge. On the other hand, natural judgment by itself does not suffice; it must be nurtured from without:

ainsi les pieces empruntées d'autruy, il les transformera et confondera, pour en faire un ouvrage tout sien, à sçavoir son jugement. Son institution, son travail et estude ne vise qu'à le former (I, 26, 151).

There seems to be a semantic shift involved; the faculty of "jugement naturel" is able to discern and deduce. In the second passage, "à sçavoir son jugement," judgment appears to be a quality, an ability which grows and is formed through all that it assimilates. Since "la verité et la raison" (I, 26, 150) are the goals of judgment, judgment must be, in a sense, the manifestation of truth and reason within the individual or at least an inclination towards the search for truth and reason. Hence, the question when judgment is a faculty and when it is a quality is not a simple one.[2] Perhaps Van den Bruwaene is right to state that "le jugement est une sorte de vertu que l'on forme en soi; même plus, il dépend de dispositions naturelles, qu'il nous reste à développer en nous, à fortifier." [3]

Montaigne speaks highly of his father's natural abilities. Pierre Eyquem, "homme, pour n'estre aydé que de l'experience et du naturel, d'un jugement bien net" (I, 35, 220), is able to judge clearly because natural propensities and experience have been successfully combined within his person. Experience does not come of its own accord; it must be actively sought. The "vulgaire," the common herd, differ from the enlightened humanists in this one important respect; the latter knowingly give themselves to experience as a means to obtain wisdom:

[1] I, 50, 289 and I, 26, 145.

[2] Indeed, it is difficult at times to distinguish the act from the faculty: "Voylà des traits bien hazardeux, selon mon jugement" (II, 33, 710).

[3] Van den Bruwaene, p. 505.

Laissons là le peuple ... qui ne se sent point, qui ne se juge point, qui laisse la plus part de ses facultez naturelles oisives. Je veux prendre l'homme en sa plus haute assiette. Considerons le en ce petit nombre d'hommes excellens et triez qui, ayant esté douez d'une belle et particuliere force naturelle, l'ont encore roidie et esguisée par soin, par estude et par art, et l'ont montée au plus haut point de sagesse où elle puisse atteindre (II, 12, 481).

Although the general context of the "Apologie" leaves no doubt that the "force naturelle" which Montaigne has in mind is reason, it is interesting to note that the verbs *roidir* and *esguiser* are verbs which not only denote the malleability of reason but also connote the emerging emphasis which Montaigne will place on two important realms of judgment, the intellectual (*esguiser*) and the moral (*roidir*).

Formal education is relegated to a secondary role: "Je m'attens qu'elle serve d'ornement, non de fondement" (I, 26, 151). The child's judgment must be *ébranlé*, violently jostled, in order to learn and grow. Judgment must not only be *branlé*, that is moved, set in motion; it must also be *ébranlé* [1] so that it becomes an embroiled combatant exposed to the problems of everyday life: "Or, à cet apprentissage, tout ce qui se presente à nos yeux sert de livre suffisant" (I, 26, 151).

Montaigne's educational goal is the expansion of man's horizons through the study of man and the whole of life:

A cette cause, le commerce des hommes y est merveilleusement propre, et la visite des pays estrangers (I, 26, 152).

Au nostre, un cabinet, un jardin, la table et le lit, la solitude, la compaignie, le matin et le vespre, toutes heures luy seront unes, toutes places luy seront estude; car la philosophie, qui, comme formatrice des jugements et des meurs, sera sa principale leçon, a ce privilege de se mesler par tout (I, 26, 164).

Il se tire une merveilleuse clarté, pour le jugement humain, de la frequentation du monde (I, 26, 156).

En cette eschole du commerce des hommes ... (I, 26, 153).

Although curiosity should lead man into all fields of endeavor, "qu'on luy mette en fantasie une honeste curiosité de s'enquerir de toutes choses" (I, 26, 155), one must not lose sight of the fact that man's principal subject of study is man himself: "Ce grand monde, que les uns multiplient encore comme especes soubs un genre, c'est le miroüer où il nous faut regarder pour nous connoistre de bon biais" (I, 26, 157). The formation and attainment of judgment is the goal of education. One perfects one's

[1] The following quotation is a significant exception to Bowman's thesis (*Montaigne: Essays* p. 28) that *ébranler*, as opposed to *branler*, in matters of movement and change, connotes for Montaigne unruly, unwarranted, and therefore nefarious motion: "Je voudrois que le Paluël ou Pompée, ces beaux danseurs de mon temps, apprinsent des caprioles à les voir seulement faire, sans nous bouger de nos places, comme ceux-cy veulent instruire notre entendement, sans l'esbranler" (I, 26, 151).

judgment only by studying man. Therefore, the development of judgment and the study of human nature are inseparable. One must "practice" man in order to know him, for one cannot "apprendre à bien juger et à bien parler, sans nous exercer ny à parler, ny à juger" (I, 26, 151). Knowledge of man depends upon judgment; hence, to judge is to probe, to test the myriad fluctuations within man: "Il sondera la portée d'un chacun" (I, 26, 155).

In order to test, to judge properly, one must have learned how to observe, but one cannot be merely a spectator. Observation in Montaigne is never passive; observation constitutes a willful and active participation on the part of the individual. Judgment must be constantly in action. The significance of various incidents and the importance of psychological manifestations which occur daily are not immediately discernible. As Lanson remarks, "encore est-il besoin de s'être donné, ou d'avoir reçu, une certaine formation, d'avoir pris certaines habitudes intellectuelles." [1]

It is important that man cultivate efficient and fruitful methods of observation, for the act of judging is not a mere exercise in intellectual alertness and awareness. Because the acts of judgment should enhance and transform man, it is necessary that he educate judgment carefully, for amelioration comes about in direct proportion to the means employed. Man's intent in estimating the worth of another man's life should be for purposes of self-improvement: "... regarder comment et pourquoy chaque chose se faict, et estre spectateurs de la vie des autres hommes, pour en juger et regler la leur" (I, 26, 157–158). *Juger* and *régler* become inseparable actions for Montaigne; one automatically leads to the other. Although an acute awareness of diversity may be one of Montaigne's most readily recognizable traits, he attempts nonetheless to establish order whenever and wherever he can. It was his search for order that led him to conclude that diversity best described man. *Régler* connotes both the establishment of order and the patterning of one's life after that order. Hence, man judges man in order to create himself; he imposes unity of being and an identity upon that which previously existed in unrelated parts. Thibaudet has aptly remarked that "Montaigne ne rédige pas comme les Port-Royalistes cartésiens un *Art de Penser*, mais un *art de se penser*." [2] The act of judgment is a bringing together, a solidifying of the personality; its

[1] Gustave Lanson, *Les Essais de Montaigne* (Paris, 1930), p. 167.

[2] Albert Thibaudet, "Le Quadricentenaire d'un philosophe," *La Revue de Paris*, 40 (1933), 762.

purpose is the improvement of the judge. Man is to be guided by what he finds to be worthy in another human being's life and actions.

Keen observation is a prerequisite to mature judgment, for a man's judgment is no better than his information. A "tête bien pleine," that is one which is full of proper knowledge, can be a powerful aid to a "tête bien faite." In "De l'institution des enfans," Montaigne is particularly concerned with the kind of information imparted to the child and the development of habitual reflection. In fact, the goal of Montaigne's pedagogy is the formation of an individual for whom it is habit to reflect constantly; this tense intellectual discipline is entrusted to the faculty of judgment.

Reflection is never a hasty endeavor. The faculty of judgment operates cautiously and methodically. In war, for example, one weighs many factors before making a decision: "le jugement de la valeur et foiblesse du lieu se prend par l'estimation et contrepois des forces qui l'assaillent" (I, 15, 69). The noun *contrepois* underlines the idea of *peser* (literally, *to weigh* and figuratively, *to ponder, to dwell upon*) inherent in all activities of judgment. Judgment, as a quality, is a reflective, steady, and direct approach to all matters; it is a poised and consistent method of confronting things. It often serves as a restraining force upon the lighter, quicker, and more agile reason and *discours*. In "Des cannibales," wives, out of solicitude for their husbands, endeavor to surround themselves with as many female friends as they can. Conscious that this activity, as well as many others which are not practiced in the "civilized" world, lends itself to misinterpretation, Montaigne stresses the abilities and the natural soundness of the cannibals "afin qu'on ne pense point que tout cecy se face par une simple et servile obligation à leur usance et par l'impression de l'authorité de leur ancienne coustume, sans discours et sans jugement" (I, 31, 212). *Discours* or reasoning implies discursive reason, whereas *jugement* establishes the tone and the pattern of the inquiry. It is the inquisitiveness and reflective power of judgment which question custom and convention.

When Montaigne speaks of the training of judgment, he often implies the formation of taste, style, manner or *goût* and the attainment and maintenance of a *juste mesure:*

> Après qu'on luy aura dict ce qui sert à le faire plus sage et meilleur, on l'entretiendra que c'est que Logique, Physique, Geometrie, Rhetorique; et la science qu'il choisira, ayant des-jà le jugement formé, il en viendra bien tost à bout (I, 26, 159).

The 1580 and 1582 editions read "ayant des-ja goust et jugement formé"; the 1588 edition added only the article *le* before *goust*. It seems likely that Montaigne suppressed *goust* after 1588 because he felt that the notion was inherent in the word *jugement*. Also, the sequence of ideas in the above quotation demonstrates that judgment is the center of wisdom and goodness and that one of its primary functions is the pursuit of that which will make it wiser and better. In the study of a poem, Montaigne relegates rhythm to the role of the versifier and "les inventions ... l'esprit et le jugement" (I, 26, 170) to the poet. A good poet is not necessarily a good versifier. Judgment refers to the wise and tasteful selection and presentation of subject matter. In the course of the (B) additions, Montaigne appends a quotation from Horace's *Satires*: "Emunctae naris, durus componere versus"; "Son goût est délicat, mais ses vers raboteux." [1] When Montaigne asks that the child be judged according to whether "il a du jugement et de la grace en son parler" (I, 26, 167), or when he surveys the educational attitude of his day which stresses "science" but "du jugement et de la vertu, peu de nouvelles" (I, 25, 135), he gives judgment a connotation usually assigned to the seventeenth-century or classical notion of *goût*. Judgment, for Montaigne, often borders on the *je ne sais quoi*, that unfathomable but recognizable manifestation of truth and genius. The *juste milieu* praised by the seventeenth-century "honnête homme" is present in Montaigne's equation of *jugement* and *goût*.

Judgment is also the cumulative total of man's digested experience. The more he uses his "estamine," the more he grows in stature. Judgment thrives upon exercise; in fact, it has been said that "il n'y a de jugement que dans l'exercice du jugement, de pensée que dans l'exercice de la pensée. Et c'est cet exercice même qui compte, nullement les résultats, lesquels ne sont jamais assurés." [2] Although Montaigne expects improvements within the moral realm of judgment, exercise for the sake of exercise is a fairly good statement of Montaigne's attitude towards judgment. Sound judgment hinges upon the constant alertness of the "facultés naturelles." It is for this reason that Montaigne heaps anecdote upon anecdote and fact upon fact, not facetiously, but because they do exist.

The sixteenth century was overwhelmed by ideas and knowledge, and Montaigne was aware of the need to find or develop some sort of

[1] Trans. Albert Thibaudet.

[2] Sylvestre De Sacy, "Montaigne essaie ses facultés naturelles," *Mercure de France*, 315 (1952), 304.

rule or method whereby one could control the truth or falsehood of knowledge and experience. Accordingly, he urges that the child be subjected to "cette diversité de jugemens: il choisira s'il peut, sinon il en demeurera en doubte" (I, 26, 150). In this instance, the *jugemens* are the "principles" set forth by Aristotle, the Stoics, and the Epicureans. Montaigne stresses the exercise of choice, for without it, there can be no true or relatively true knowledge, only an accumulation of facts and information. The exercise of judgment is an act of "triage," and the verb *trier* occurs frequently in the *Essais*.

Montaigne moves easily from soul to *jugement:* "Si nostre ame n'en va un meilleur bransle, si nous n'en avons le jugement plus sain ..." (I, 25, 137). Although he emphasizes the need to train the soul and the body concomitantly, for they must be treated as one, he seems to feel that the soul is the more important of the two. Certainly, when ill-formed or unbalanced, it causes more havoc than the body. Throughout "Du pedantisme" and "De l'institution des enfans," he stresses at times the amelioration of the soul and at others that of judgment; there seems to be more parallelism involved between soul and judgment than between judgment and any other faculty. Perhaps Montaigne finds it difficult to separate one from the other because of the great significance which he attributes to both. He associates judgment with the moral realm, as readily as he does the soul. More and more, his educational program stresses the evolution of the spiritual nature of man: "Le guain de nostre estude, c'est en estre devenu meilleur et plus sage" (I, 26, 151).

Emphasis on wisdom and goodness delineates the moral aspect of judgment. The preceptor is asked to teach the child, not histories *per se*, but the ability to judge them, because Montaigne feels that the important aspect of education is the acquisition of the capacity to decipher and determine the moral worth of man. The faculty of judgment must be able to determine good and evil, truth and falsehood, in men and in their actions. Hence, to judge is to seek moral and psychological knowledge: "pour Montaigne, jugement signifie presque toujours *jugement moral*: sa critique ne s'applique pas tant à connaître *la réalité véritable* des choses qu'à saisir la probité des actes et la véracité des caractères." [1]

For Montaigne, the goal of education is the liberation of man: "Une bonne institution, elle change le jugement et les meurs" (II, 17, 644).

[1] F. J. Billeskov Jansen, *Sources vives de la pensée de Montaigne: Etude sur les fondements psychologiques et biographiques des Essais* (Copenhagen, 1935), p. 23.

Morally and intellectually independent through the faculty of judgment, man can hope to rise above his original condition. There can be no greater asset for man than the faculty of judgment, for "it is the part of man that teaches him how to live." [1]

OPERATION OF JUDGMENT

When Montaigne declares that a good education transforms man's judgment, he is referring to the problem of human knowledge. In the "Apologie de Raimond Sebond," he remarks that man obtains all knowledge through his senses. All that one can know is acquired by "la faculté du cognoissant"; since "le jugement vient de l'operation de celuy qui juge," it behooves man to improve this operation (II, 12, 571–572). Judgment seems to be equated with knowledge or the search for knowledge in such a way that it is necessary to assume that the faculty of judgment is the seat or storehouse of knowledge. Furthermore, the relationship of *jugement* and *juger* leaves no doubt that it is the faculty of judgment which is understood whenever the verb *juger* appears. In other words, however Montaigne uses the verb *juger*, that is "je juge," meaning Montaigne, or "ils jugent," meaning others, one must assume in all cases that it is the faculty of judgment which is in action.

If, as it seems to be, judgment is both "connaissance" and a "recherche de la connaissance," and if the senses, as Montaigne states elsewhere, are the first judges, one can glimpse the physical underpinnings of judgment. How the senses relate their information to the judgment is a complicated, and as yet unexplored, subject. Nevertheless, a faculty can be defined by its role, operation, and object. The object of judgment is human knowledge in all of its forms, that is psychic, moral, and physical or material. Only divine knowledge escapes or should escape its surveillance and scrutiny.

Montaigne knows that absolute knowledge is either inexistent or unattainable. At best, knowledge is a subjective entity, for its "essence" is assimilated differently by one and all. Yet, men of good judgment must be able to agree somehow on relative truths. In their exuberance over newly acquired erudition, Montaigne's sixteenth-century predecessors were content to publicize their discoveries, oblivious to contradictions and blatant fallacies. Knowledge, that is *savoir* rather than *connaissance*, for the sake of knowledge was the order of the day.

[1] Frame, *Montaigne's Discovery of Man*, p. 80.

Montaigne felt that some means of separating fact from fiction, truth from falsehood had to be devised or man would become sterile. No doubt, Montaigne himself compiled and catalogued anecdotes without distinction in his first essays; however, in his later years, he recognized that many of his early essays imitated too servilely the methods of his models: "aucuns puent un peu à l'estranger" (III, 5, 853).

Intelligence, reason, and memory are the faculties most responsible for man's chaotic state. Memory in and of itself is useless; it belongs to the past, and it cannot always be trusted; Montaigne admits to having been a victim of its treachery. Reason seems to have no past; it operates in the present. It encroaches upon the future in that it often gets ahead of itself, usually by means of syllogisms. Together, reason and memory have left man debilitated. Only the faculty of judgment spans man's temporality; within it are contained past, present, and future, past because it is the product of all that it has encountered, present since its role is a daily and constant guidance of man, and future because it strives, on the basis of past and present experience, for his moral betterment.

If judgment is to do for man all that Montaigne asks of it, it is evident that its mode of operation will be a cautious, ponderous, and skeptical one. Its task is a conscious, painstaking, and thorough analysis of all its objects. This is not a simple matter, for Montaigne finds inconstancy more prevalent than constancy. Since the objects of judgment's study are continually in motion and undergoing change, judgment, itself subject to inconstancy and indecision, must deal with infinitely minute occurrences. The role of judgment is to judge "en destail et distinctement piece à piece" (II, 1, 316). Everything is to be separated into its component parts and evaluated.

Basically, judgment is intelligence, the ability to think, and it is in this sense that Montaigne applies it to his discussion of animal behavior in the "Apologie de Raimond Sebond": "Les arondelles ... cherchent elles sans jugement et choisissent elles sans discretion, de mille places, celle qui leur est la plus commode à se loger?" (II, 12, 432). In this case, choice is a matter of discernment, of discrimination; *jugement*, like "discretion," is a quality, an ability; it is specifically the thinking process.[1] When an animal builds a circular structure rather than a

[1] "Comme faisoient aux chiens les Espaignols à la nouvele conqueste des Indes, ausquels ils payoient solde et faisoient partage au butin; et montroient ces animaux autant d'adresse et de jugement à poursuivre et arrester leur victoire, à charger ou à reculer selon les occasions, à distinguer les amis des ennemis, comme ils faisoient d'ardeur et d'aspreté" (II, 12, 445).

square one, or when it cushions its lair with moss and down for the comfort of its young, is it not demonstrating "deliberation, et pensement, et conclusion?" (II, 12, 432). Inference, thought, and reflection are the basic attributes of judgment. Whenever one espies a conscious choice or whenever, as in the case of animals, one considers one action to be preferable to or more reasonable than another, one is witnessing the effect of judgment.

Although the idea of discernment and of discrimination constitutes an inherent part of judgment, it is remarkable that Montaigne so often states it separately. The people who witness a heated discussion often give the advantage to the wrong person, for the public is "communément foible et incapable de bien juger et discerner les vrays avantages" (III, 8, 917). No doubt, *discerner* distends the effect of *juger*. However, one would expect *discerner* to precede *juger*, since *juger* is considered to be the more general term and *discerner* but a step within the process of judgment. In such occurrences, it may be that *juger* specifically connotes "connaître" and "déterminer"; in this case, *juger* would refer to the establishment and recognition of what the advantages of the discussion might have been and *discerner* would imply not scrutiny but the choice of the "vrays avantages." At times, *juger* seems to be equated with *voir* and *jugement* with *vue;* hence, in cases where *juger* is further qualified by another verb, it might be plausible to conceive of the qualifier as the pertinent aspect of the sentence or action and of *juger* as the notion of "arrêter," "déterminer," "voir," or "connaître." Certainly, the conjunction of the two verbs creates the impression that Montaigne perhaps conceives of them as representative of two separate actions. The word *vrays* indicates the primary purpose of the act of judgment. One judges in order to establish truth; judgment scorns futile intellectualizing.

At times, the distending effect brought about by the accumulation of synonyms or of meaningful parts of the verb *juger* is far more extensive. In "Des vaines subtilitez," Montaigne establishes a three-stage continuum upon which he divides humanity as it is seen in its response to human suffering. Stupidity and wisdom are alike ("se rencontrent en mesme point") in that neither suffers. The stupid man ignores suffering and, hence, is at one end of the continuum ("au deçà des accidens") while the wise man, by means of conscious courage, ascends above it and takes his place at the other extreme ("au delà"). The bulk of humanity finds itself midway between both extremes: "l'ordinaire et moyenne condition des hommes loge entre ces deux extremitez, qui est de ceux qui apperçoivent les maux, les sentent, et ne les peuvent supporter" (I, 54, 299). The wise men are the only ones who have reflected upon their state of suffering and attempted to transcend it: "après en avoir bien poisé et consideré les qualitez, les avoir mesurez et jugez tels qu'ils sont, [ils] s'eslancent au-dessus par la force d'un vigoureux courage." It is interesting to note that "bien poisé et consideré" and "mesurez" are all involved in the process of judging and, consequently, redundant. On the other hand, it can be accepted that to judge is the final act in this vigorous process of inquiry of which truth is always the goal: "tels qu'ils sont." Common man does not weigh, consider, measure, and judge experience; he is merely a sentient creature.

The act of judgment is a deliberative process in which organization, judgment, and choice play separate parts. A subordinate should always represent things to his superior in such a way that "la liberté d'ordonner, juger et choisir demeurast au maistre" (I, 17, 73). However, to judge infers "ordonner" and "choisir"; perhaps, to ponder (*peser*) and to reflect best convey the meaning of *juger* in this sentence. Yet, in the "Apologie," Montaigne states that the Pyrrhonists use their reason "pour enquerir et pour debatre, mais non pas pour arrester et choisir" (II, 12, 485). They attempt to maintain "un jugement sans pente et sans inclination." The role of reason would seem to be that of inquiry and debate while that of judgment appears to be that of arbitration or judging. Reason is cast in the role of contending lawyers. The parallel structure in both sentences, that is "juger et choisir" and "arrester et choisir," indicates that "juger" and "arrester" are synonymous on several levels. "Arrêter" infers a stoppage of the discursive and endless movement. No doubt, its legal connotation of "to decree" is pertinent in this case. For Montaigne, *juger* and time are never far apart. He attaches judgments to temporality; things come to a stop, cease to function; in a sense, the faculty of judgment always brings something to a close. There is a finality, although a momentary one since flux governs everything, about each passing judgment.

In "Du parler prompt ou tardif," Montaigne aligns preachers with the faculty of judgment and lawyers with the mind (*esprit*). The intricacies and accidents of the advocate's profession require agility and resilience of mind. On the contrary, the faculty of judgment is more suited to the preacher, for more leisure time is available to him; he can sit and think without interruption. The lawyer's task is the more difficult one; yet, in France, there are fewer good preachers than lawyers. It seems that the mind, whether it represents the intellectual aspect of the soul or the soul in its entirety, is a more natural or innate faculty; if you possess it, its operation is automatic; it perceives and acts upon relationships instinctively. The speed with which it operates leaves little room for meditation: "Il semble que ce soit plus le propre de l'esprit d'avoir son operation prompte et soudaine, et plus le propre du jugement de l'avoir lente et posée" (I, 10, 41). The productions of the mind are somewhat more fortuitous; judgment depends on personal "diligence."

The faculty of judgment comprises a "vehemente premeditation et laborieuse." Its employment demands great effort, which is perhaps the reason for its lack of use. The operation of judgment is slow because the objects or questions which it treats are more important ones. The word *posée* (deliberate, composed, grave) implies a conscious germination, a building process, which leads to "mieux dire" (I, 10, 41), that is the demonstration of superior thought, of judgment.

Montaigne argues that his "facultez naturelles" are not equal to their task, for "mes conceptions et mon jugement ne marche qu'à tastons, chancelant, bronchant et chopant" (I, 26, 145). The vivid description of judgment's chaotic course would tend to minimize the significance and effectiveness of such a faculty. Nevertheless, it is apparent that this is its role. Montaigne intends that the reader visualize the creative process, for, in a very real sense, the *Essais* come into being by means of the struggle between Montaigne's judgment and the body of knowledge which it activates. Montaigne neither is unduly humble nor does he misinterpret the difficulty of his undertaking. He knows that certain things escape him: "je voy encore du païs au delà, mais d'une veuë trouble et en nuage, que je ne puis desmeler" (I, 26, 145). As he has stated elsewhere, it is an effect of judgment that he can acknowledge his shortcomings. More importantly, this admission disassociates judgment from the faculty which perceives or illuminates what judgment cannot fathom; this faculty is *entendement,* in the sense of intelligence, *appréhension,* or *intelligence.* Judgment gropes for an understanding because it must interpret all that is relayed to it. It is interesting to note the alliance which Montaigne forms between "conceptions" and "jugement." It is doubtful that he conceives of the faculty of judgment as the originator of ideas; rather, he believes that judgment is the conveyor of ideas, testing their value against that of others.

In" De l'institution des enfans," there are two consecutive and noteworthy suppressions of *jugement* which further describe its attributes and mode of operation. In both examples, *jugement* was eliminated after 1588. Originally, one read: "Ce que je voyois, je le voyois d'un jugement bien seur et ouvert" (I, 26, 174); this statement was altered to read "Ce que je voyois, je le voyois bien." [1] As was noted earlier, *jugement* and *voir* often appear together; the demonstration of judgment is not only a way of looking at things, but also a perception, an awareness of things. The verb *voir*, in this context, connotes "to grasp," "to understand"; one is tempted to add "to seize," with all that its literal meaning implies, for there seems to be a physical dimension to Montaigne's thought. In other words, thought, or rather judgment, can activate the physical, intellectual, and moral world and control it. Indeed, throughout "De l'institution des enfans" and "Du pedantisme," one encounters numerous images of eating, devouring, and digesting.

The role of judgment is to see, seize, and fix in time mental and physical phenomena. The adjectives *seur* and *ouvert* infer that in Montaigne's case judgment was able to capture phenomena "en leur vray estre," and ascertain its true meaning and worth. Moreover, the elimination of *jugement* strengthens the guiding force of the "je" to the extent that the "je" and judgment appear to be synonymous. The problem of the directing "je" or "moi," as Frame calls it,[2] is an exciting and highly complicated one; it is directly related to the problem of the psyche, and an initial tabulation of several examples indicates that the faculty of judgment and the directing "je" are usually identical.[3]

The second suppression of *jugement*, which immediately precedes the former, pertains to a eulogy of Montaigne's father. The elder Montaigne had attempted to enliven the study of Greek by turning it into a game and had ordered that Michel be awakened by the sound of music rather than by sudden and violent means so that he would not become addle-brained, as was held by contemporary lore. Montaigne concludes that "cet exemple suffira pour en juger le reste, et pour recommander aussi et la prudence et l'affection d'un si bon pere" (I, 26, 174). The term *prudence* replaced *jugement*; the juxtaposition of *jugement*, *prudence*, and *affection* suggests that, in this context, *jugement* is a quality and that *prudence*, as a substitute for *jugement*, is an accurate and significant synonym. Prudence, in the words of Webster's New International

[1] Because of the general context of "De l'institution des enfans," it is likely that Montaigne also omits *jugement* in order to strengthen the premise, elaborated throughout this essay, that judgment must be trained and that it is not simply natural.

[2] Frame, "What Next in Montaigne Studies?," *French Review*, XXXVI (1963), 583.

[3] This question will be treated more fully in Chapter III, "Judgment and Being."

Dictionary, "implies caution, circumspection, or economy, esp. in the practical affairs of life." *Prudence* can be equated with *foresight,* that is "prudent care for the future." Hence, the substitution of *prudence* for *jugement* affords another insight into the meaning of *jugement* for Montaigne. Although the history of *prudentia* is notoriously problematic,[1] perhaps the most important word in the above definition is *practical.* In Montaigne's context, the demonstration of judgment implies that one is practically wise. Judgment is a prudent faculty, that is knowledgeable, cautious, and practical; these attributes make judgment the appropriate faculty to mold the self according to its nature, as Montaigne understands the term in "Nature est un doux guide" (III, 13, 1094).

Another function of judgment is found in its ability, or what should be its ability, to eliminate the incidental and non-essential aspects of its encounters. Judgment strives for brevity and conciseness; it endeavors to control and direct man's more prolific and less manageable faculties. In so far as it functions for the benefit of persons other than the proprietor, it can be considered as a social faculty. When associating with others, man must allow himself to be guided by judgment, that is a certain sort of "savoir-faire." In conversation, as in "Des menteurs" (I, 9, 35–36), man's judgment should tell him what is appropriate and necessary and what is offensive and superfluous. Whether telling a story or passing on information, one must not allow memory to hinder one's effectiveness. Judgment must make one speak directly with little deviation. Judgment's infelicity comes from its inability or unwillingness to separate the circumstantial and unnecessary from the useful and the pertinent:

> Cela mesme de luy voir trier une legiere action en la vie d'un homme, ou un mot, qui semble ne porter pas: cela, c'est un discours. C'est dommage que les gens d'entendement ayment tant la briefveté; sans doute leur reputation en vaut mieux, mais nous en valons moins; Plutarque aime mieux que nous le vantions de son jugement que de son sçavoir; il ayme mieux nous laisser desir de soy que satieté. Il sçavoit qu'és choses bonnes mesmes on peut trop dire (I, 26, 156).

No doubt, the "gens d'entendement" are the precursors of the "honnêtes hommes," who dare not be experts in any subject, who touch upon any and all topics, and who pride themselves in their attitude of

[1] *Prudentia* is the sagacious conduct of life, according to the laws of God, thanks to the control of being by just reason. It is wisdom shown in the exercise of reason, and it is only later that it acquires the notions of cautious, practical. For a detailed and very competent history of the concept of wisdom in the Renaissance, see Eugene F. Rice, Jr., *The Renaissance Idea of Wisdom* (Cambridge, 1958).

"ne se piquer de rien." Montaigne's "gens d'entendement" and "honnêtes hommes" demonstrate in all things an "esprit de finesse" and not an "esprit de géométrie." The role of judgment is to snatch, pick out (*trier*), deductively and intuitively, unobtrusive pieces of information and analyze and display them for what they are. *Trier*, in this passage, implies more than the separation of one thing from another; in this instance, Montaigne infers to uncover, to discover, to ferret out. One can present an entire "discours" based on a rather insignificant action, and, as Montaigne points out, a judicious person, such as Plutarch, will content himself with letting the reader elaborate the "discours" and, descriptively, put it "en place marchande." In this example, Plutarch's *jugement* is the quality of being able to select *the* significant aspect of a man's life, the one which, no matter how trivial, leads to the best moral evaluation of the man.

The importance of choice and its exercise in Montaigne's teleology has already been discussed. For Montaigne, choice, an act of judgment, implies superiority; by definition, anything one does by choice is superior to all other forms of action and thought. Friendship far outweighs love because man is not driven to it by some irresistible and uncontrollable impulse; likewise, a friend is better than a brother, for a friend is chosen. To choose or to judge is so important that Montaigne would rather have one judge badly than not judge at all.

In "De la ressemblance des enfans aux peres," Montaigne insists that he always tries to explain and accept or reject whatever natural propensities he finds within himself. He ponders his dislike of the medical profession and wonders if it is not the result of a family tradition. He seeks the true motive behind natural inclinations, "car toutes ces conditions qui naissent en nous sans raison, elles sont vitieuses, c'est une espece de maladie qu'il faut combatre" (II, 37, 743). One must examine all manifestations, retaining or rejecting them as judgment ordains. Judgment is the faculty which enables man to rise above his condition. Man can be what he must choose to be "par jugement et liberté volontaire" (II, 8, 366). All natural inclinations must be judged, even the love of parents for their children: "J'ay, de ma part, le goust estrangement mousse à ces propensions qui sont produites en nous sans l'ordonnance et entremise de nostre jugement" (II, 8, 366). Hence, nature is best manifested through judgment. The faculty of judgment must govern and control all the complex emotions which motivate man.

The faculty of judgment is constantly probing man and itself. In other words, judgment is aware of its own activity; it should admonish itself when it attempts to overstep its authority or when it shirks its duty. More importantly, unlike the other faculties, it should be keenly cognizant of its own strengths and weaknesses and be willing to admit them to itself: "il eschape souvent des fautes à nos yeux, mais la maladie du jugement consiste à ne les pouvoir apercevoir lorsqu'un autre nous les descouvre" (II, 10, 388). To discover and to confess one's mistakes constitutes "un effet de jugement et de sincerité, qui sont les principales parties qu'il cherche" (I, 26, 154).

Judgment operates both outwardly and inwardly on others and on oneself; it knows that the individual is never far from repeating past mistakes or making new ones; it endeavors to remind man, at every step of the way, that much introspection and improvement remain to be undertaken. Its role is to ferret out faults and vices wherever it finds them and to accuse the perpetrators: "j'entens que nostre jugement, chargeant sur un autre duquel pour lors il est question, ne nous espargne pas d'une interne jurisdiction" (III, 8, 908). A man cannot publicly glorify his wife's background while deriding another man's habit of incessantly brandishing his genealogies; one is no less "intemperant et ennuyeus" than the other. Hence, judgment must not only mediate man's propensities but also uncover and eradicate his bad habits, a function which is that of judgment alone, not of conscience. When we say "I could kick myself for having spoken to him that way," one is conceptualizing a duality of being; the superior "I" oversees the activities of the self and strives to have it abide by its standards. For Montaigne, judgment is the "I," the directing "je."

Judgment does not come under the control of any other faculty. Montaigne gives it priority in all things and assigns to it the responsibility of governing him in every action:

> Le jugement tient chez moy un siege magistral, au moins il s'en efforce soingneusement; il laisse mes appetis aller leur trein, et la haine et l'amitié, voire et celle que je me porte à moy-mesme, sans s'en alterer et corrompre. S'il ne peut reformer les autres parties selon soy, au moins ne se laisse il pas difformer à elles: il faict son jeu à part (III, 13, 1052).

Judgment is an authority unto itself. Its strength lies in its ability to deal with man's fancies and desires ("appetis"), seeing and evaluating them for what they are, without abetting them or becoming imbued with them. Montaigne may think highly of himself; yet his judgment will not allow him to do so when there is no cause. The faculty of judgment does not deceive itself; subject and object never become one. It never loses sight of its role and of the standards which it alone establishes. The verb *reformer* stresses the constant pressure which it brings to bear on the self. Judgment is the faculty that strives to turn man into as perfect a being as he can be.

Man must always be aware that his role in life is no more than a role and must not allow his official function to become a part of the self: "Il faut jouer deuement nostre rolle, mais comme rolle d'un personnage emprunté" (III, 10, 989). It is judgment that enables Montaigne to remain aloof from the Mayor. Judgment seeks the truth of the self, and it can only be found within the self:

le jugement d'un Empereur doit estre au dessus de son empire, et le voir et considerer comme accident estranger; et luy, doit sçavoir jouyr de soy à part et se communicquer comme Jacques et Pierre, au moins à soymesmes (III, 10, 989).

The emperor must be cognizant that his imperial power comes not from within but from the position he holds through an accident of birth. Judgment controls man's propensity toward self-illusion. Since its primary function is the search for truth, it must also keep in check man's tendency toward self-hatred and self-depreciation. Man must see himself for what he is, neither worse nor better than he is capable of judging: "Le jugement doit tout par tout maintenir son droit: c'est raison qu'il voye en ce subject, comme ailleurs, ce que la verité luy presente" (II, 17, 615). Judgment must divorce itself from everything which surrounds it while actively engaged in judging all that it encounters. Montaigne sets an arduous course for judgment.

In his discussion of the Pyrrhonists, Montaigne is particularly concerned with the faculty of judgment; his advocation of Pyrrhonism does not imply a deep personal, and for Montaigne unnecessary, commitment to its discipline, for he is by nature skeptical. Throughout the "Apologie de Raimond Sebond," he uses Pyrrhonism, as he would any other philosophy which might serve his purpose, to undermine man's presumption and confidence in his ability to know any and all things. The Pyrrhonists claim that man can discourse upon knowledge, agitating and debating all questions, but that he is incapable of going beyond this stage into the realm of choice and decision:

cette assiette de leur jugement, droicte et inflexible, recevant tous objets sans application et consentement, les achemine à leur Ataraxie, qui est une condition de vie paisible, rassise, exempte des agitations que nous recevons par l'impression de l'opinion et science que nous pensons avoir des choses (II, 12, 483).

The faculty of judgment under discussion is strictly an intellectual one. Indeed, whenever Montaigne mentions judgment with regard to the Pyrrhonists, one never finds it associated with the moral realm or that it has any function other than that of deciding what is true and what is false.[1] Hence, judgment tends to be equated with reason, in the positive sense of the term, whenever the subject of skepticism is involved; judgment and reason can only discourse, theorize, intellectualize.

What is noteworthy is the possibility that a faculty as limited as judgment, according to the Pyrrhonists and Montaigne in the "Apologie," can be curtailed in its activities and suspended. More importantly, who or what is empowered to limit the functioning of judgment? If judgment is suspended intellectually, what happens to the far more significant aspects of judgment which have already been discussed? If judgment cannot establish truth and falsehood, how can it differentiate between good and evil?

Si noz facultez intellectuelles et sensibles sont sans fondement et sans pied, si elles ne font que floter et vanter, pour neant laissons nous emporter nostre jugement à aucune partie de leur operation, quelque apparence qu'elle semble nous presenter(II, 12, 544–545).

This sequence of ideas illustrates the authoritative relationship of judgment with regard to the other "facultez intellectuelles et sensibles"; yet, one wonders if the faculty of judgment itself is able to withhold its participation or whether some other center of the psyche, such as the will, is at liberty to control its operation. The problem is even more clearly outlined in the following lines:

Nous autres, qui privons nostre jugement du droict de faire des arrests, regardons mollement les opinions diverses, et, si nous n'y prestons le jugement, nous y prestons aiséement l'oreille (III, 8, 901).

Perhaps, judgment polices itself; as was noted earlier, judgment, in several instances, leads one to believe that it is the directing "je." As for the various intellectual, moral, and social aspects of judgment, one must conclude that they are not interdependent and that the suspension of one function does not include the curtailment of the others.

Of course, there is a problem of chronology in Montaigne; the "philosophy" which he espouses in 1579–1580 ("De l'institution des enfans") greatly overshadows the lack of confidence in man's abilities which he professes earlier in 1575–1576 ("Apologie de Raimond

[1] "Et disoit Archesilas les soustenemens et l'estat droit et inflexible du jugement estre les biens, mais les consentements et applications estre les vices et les maux.... Les Pyrrhoniens, quand ils disent que le souverain bien c'est l'Ataraxie, qui est l'immobilité du jugement, ils ne l'entendent pas dire d'une façon affirmative" (II, 12, 562).

Sebond"). One is tempted to attribute to an evolving "philosophy" what appear to be changes and successive stages within the concept of judgment. However, by and large, there is but one highly significant and far-reaching transformation and that is Montaigne's identification of judgment with the self in the search for knowledge. Montaigne's ever-increasing confidence in the ability of judgment to raise man above his condition does not explain adequately the variations which one finds within the attributes of judgment and its mode of operation. Indeed, greater confidence in the capabilities of judgment should entail a corresponding reduction in the limitations, both constitutional and operational, of judgment.

CHAPTER II

THE LIMITATIONS OF JUDGMENT

Montaigne claims so much for the faculty of judgment that one is apt to overlook his frequent and forceful references to its follies and maladies. Montaigne finds it impossible to escape his own dictum: "Nostre vie est partie en folie, partie en prudence. Qui n'en escrit que reveremment et regulierement, il en laisse en arriere plus de la moitié" (III, 5, 866–867). No matter how strong and how well trained an individual's judgment may be, there are always moments when its ability to function properly is impaired and stifled by its constitutional inadequacies or by man's physical body and his passions. Moreover, there are domains of knowledge and experience which remain inaccessible to judgment and others which should not be allowed to come within its scrutiny.

Montaigne comes to believe that man's perfection lies within the exercise and development of his judgment. Since experience cannot be obtained in a vacuum, it is understandable that judgment will often stumble and act foolishly. However, some are greater fools than others, and one wonders if the greater or lesser degree of stupidity is not based initially on class distinctions. When Montaigne delineates his pedagogical program in "De l'institution des enfans," he does not consider that the "vulgaire" might also prove to have judgment. As Strowski remarks, "l'exercice du jugement et particulièrement du jugement moral est d'ailleurs un des privilèges et des caractères du gentilhomme."[1] In fact, the "honnête homme" can always be relied upon to demonstrate instinctively more judgment, be it only "goût" or "savoir-faire," than his less privileged fellow man.

When Montaigne speaks of the inadequacies of judgment, one is often confronted with a parallel between the "vulgaire" and the "honnête homme," for the "honnête homme," or rather the Senecan,

[1] Fortunat Strowski, *La Sagesse française* Paris, 1925), p. 101.

stoically "roide" individual, is meant to be placed and seen above the unlearned, often stupid, and always dependent "vulgaire." Left to their own devices, the "vulgaire" seem incapable of judgment; they band together and let chance decide their course. In discussing the inadequacies of their judgment, Montaigne demonstrates a keen understanding of crowd psychology. The sheep instinct, the opprobrium of judgment, is within all men. As Montaigne's knowledge of the world about him increases, he tends to soften his attack on the "vulgaire." Differences between the "honnête homme" and the "vulgaire" greatly diminish. Indeed, at times, the "vulgaire" seem to command more concern and respect. After 1588, Montaigne argues that "nous sommes tous du vulgaire" (II, 12, 554). A slow but constant leveling process marks Montaigne's journey through the years. Judgment can be uniformly stupid; occasionally, the heights of folly and vice cause more permanent havoc in the "honnête homme" than in the "vulgaire." Inasmuch as the opposition continues, although greatly abated, throughout the *Essais*, it is possible to see the emergence of a distinction of faculties where the two parties are concerned: *sens*, the great leveler, is perhaps more "vulgaire" and therefore more general than the more "honnête" *jugement*. Changes within *sens* and *jugement* and their relationship to each other as well as to other faculties will be discussed in Chapter IV, "The Relationship of Judgment to the Other Faculties."

It was noted earlier that Montaigne never ceases to berate the faculty of judgment, although he considers it man's first and most important faculty. Limitations imposed upon the concept of judgment are diachronic as well as synchronic. Moreover, certain limitations are highly significant; they point to new meanings and associations within the concept of judgment. Montaigne's recognition of the impact of the physical body, for example, upon judgment and the subsequent distortions and contortions of judgment reveal his astute awareness of modern psychosomatic theory and give greater dimension to the faculty of judgment as a prime area of the psyche.

EXALTATION AND ALTERATION

Montaigne continually stresses the advisability and necessity of acquiring and maintaining a judgment "droit" and "rassis." This "assiette" or attitude on the part of judgment enables it to acquire the intellectual and moral truth which it seeks. Judgment must test all the new appearances which it encounters in life; in fact, "rien de ce qui est humain ne doit échapper au contrôle du jugement." [1] If all man's deeds, thoughts, and emotions must pass through judgment, one would think that there should be no room for aberrations. Yet there is one which was greatly discussed by poets and other literati in the sixteenth century: "fureur divine." The inspiration of the poet, his mania or mental exaltation, was an accepted facet of his art; no one questioned it, no one denied it.[2] It was felt that the poet's inspiration escaped the bonds of reason and that it was superhuman and godlike, a "fureur divine."

The topic of mental exaltation within the poetic circles of the century is commonplace. What is significant for the study of judgment is the fact that Montaigne himself considers that truth can be found, not only through the possession and production of judgment, but also through a certain "élan," indeed through the annihilation or collapse of judgment. In "De la phisionomie," Montaigne compares Seneca's method of preparing himself for death to that of Plutarch. He prefers Plutarch's approach, which deals with death disdainfully, to Seneca's, who is forever in fear of death and contrives consciously and assiduously to make himself equal to the task of dying. Montaigne can appreciate both attitudes, but the reasonableness of Plutarch outweighs the overwhelming aspect of Seneca's position:

> L'un, plus vif, nous pique et eslance en sursaut, touche plus l'esprit. L'autre, plus rassis, nous informe, establit et conforte constamment, touche plus l'entendement. (C) Celuy là ravit nostre jugement, cestuy-cy le gaigne (III, 12, 1017).

Apart from the fact in the (C) addition that Montaigne seems to have suppressed the juxtaposition of *esprit* and *entendement* in favor of a more general distinction on the plane of judgment, the significance of these lines lies perhaps in the verbs *ravir* and *gagner*. Because the *esprit-entendement-jugement* triangle is reduced to one faculty by the post–1588 addition, it seems legitimate to link the description of *esprit* with *ravir* and that of *entendement* with *gagner*. The idea of prickling and startling does not clash with *ravir*; it appropriately describes the reaction of the mind to outside stimuli; it is a reaction which Montaigne consistently assigns to the mind. On the other hand, *entendement*, the obvious equal of judgment in this instance, is a far more stable and sedate faculty, one which reacts more organically and profoundly to

[1] Albert Peyre, *Du Prestige de la pensée* (Paris, 1936), pp. 229–230.

[2] The role of the poet's divine inspiration does not prevail until 1550. See Robert V. Merrill with Robert J. Clements, *Platonism in French Renaissance Poetry* (New York, 1957) and particularly "The Four Furies," pp. 118–144.

appearances, as the verb *informer* indicates; *entendement-jugement* is formed, but more importantly, it is won over, persuaded ("le *gaigne*"), and, one surmises, by the strength and worth of the argument.

Judgment always lets itself be persuaded by the truth or at least it should. Montaigne does not seriously believe that one's judgment can be suspended, at least not in matters where relative knowledge is the object and judgment finds itself in a position of "pente" and "inclination," based on long and well-recorded experience. Judgment must choose; yet one finds that judgment can be both forced (or raped) and won over. Where judgment is concerned, *ravir* and *gagner* are identical; hence, Seneca and Plutarch carry equal force, according to the judgment. Judgment espies the truth of both positions; yet it cannot always deal with it rationally; at times, it will allow itself to be guided or rather forced by instinct, mental exaltation, and alteration. As Van den Bruwaene remarks, "le jugement rassis n'est tout de même pas la norme absolue; il y a place encore pour des éclats." [1]

Montaigne's major statement on the effect of poetry upon man's judgment is found in a (C) addition to "Du jeune Caton":

> Voicy merveille: nous avons bien plus de poëtes, que de juges et interpretes de poësie. Il est plus aisé de la faire, que de la cognoistre. A certaine mesure basse, on la peut juger par les preceptes et par art. Mais la bonne, l'excessive, la divine est au-dessus des regles et de la raison. Quiconque en discerne la beauté d'une veuë ferme et rassise, il ne la void pas, non plus que la splendeur d'un esclair. Elle ne pratique point nostre jugement; elle le ravit et ravage (I, 37, 227–228).

The sequence and relationship of *poëtes*, *juges*, *interpretes*, *faire*, *cognoistre*, and *juger* underscore the synonymity of judging and knowing. More importantly, one can know intuitively as well as deductively. Reality is not all; the true beauty of a poem cannot be reasoned. Divine poetry is beyond judgment; when faced with it, "il s'estonnera, il se transira." Judgment abdicates; *veuë* and *void* express an exteriorization of the process of knowing. In order to know and appreciate truly inspired poetry, the faculty of judgment must be no less inspired; it is stripped ("le . . . *ravage*") of its deductive powers. No act of judgment takes place; truth and beauty make themselves manifest to the faculty of judgment in much the same way that man, for Montaigne, knows God through faith alone.

The idea of *ravir* and *ravager* adds a new dimension to the faculty of judgment, that is one of intuitive and superintellectual knowledge. Mental exaltation does not constitute a limitation upon the activities of

[1] Van den Bruwaene, p. 511.

judgment; on the contrary, it enhances them. However, where judgment is concerned, mental exaltation is disagreeable; judgment likes to remain in control of itself and ecstasy is not a rational act. In order to be overwhelmed as it is by divine poetry, judgment must become one with the object of its analysis, an inequity which Montaigne deplores. No doubt, Montaigne recognizes the reality of various forms of "éclats"; heroism is one which frequently attracts his attention.[1] Yet, no matter how great or how legitimate such "éclats" may appear to be, he confides that Aristotle "a raison d'appeller folie tout eslancement, tant loüable soit-il, qui surpasse nostre propre jugement et discours" (II, 2, 330). The verb *surpasser* indicates the understanding and comprehensive aspect of judgment. When Montaigne refers to judgment in these passages, he does not imply an ability to discern, to judge, but a capacity to grasp, to comprehend; in these occurrences, judgment is specifically the faculty of knowing.

Judgment both receives and conceives; in the case of its "ravissement" by poetry, it receives, but does not conceive. In the last example, *jugement* is a composite faculty, which includes total mental activity; that which is beyond judgment also surpasses *raison, sens, entendement,* and *discours*. Moreover, suspension of judgment can connote madness. In "De la force de l'imagination," Montaigne remarks that "Gallus Vibius banda si bien son ame à comprendre l'essence et les mouvemens de la folie, qu'il emporta son jugement hors de son siege, si qu'onques puis il ne l'y peut remettre" (I, 21, 95). Uncontrolled imagination can be most dangerous to the proper equilibrium of the soul. Judgment is the faculty most affected by abnormal states; in fact, an abnormal mental state consists of an aberration of *jugement*. If madness is looked upon as the loss of the faculty of judgment, one must conclude that judgment is the seat of all rational mental activity.

Gallus Vibius lost his mind by means of an overly active imagination. Montaigne does not deny that it demands even less to unhinge an ordinary man's judgment:

> Ce fleuteur protocole de Gracchus, qui amolissoit, roidissoit et contournoit la vois de son maistre lors qu'il haranguoit à Rome, à quoy servoit il, si le mouvement et qualité du son n'avoit force à esmouvoir et alterer le jugement des auditeurs? Vrayement il y a bien dequoy faire si grande feste de la fermeté de cette belle piece, qui se laisse manier et changer au branle et accidens d'un si leger vent (II, 12, 580)!

[1] Montaigne readily admits that in some areas judgment itself may be transcended because he also perceives that he and his ideas, his view of life, may be transcended; his program is the best perhaps for most of us, but variations and exceptions must neither be neglected nor dismissed.

Judgment's susceptibility to the senses is one of its great weaknesses and one which impedes its orderly functioning more than any other facet of life. The effect of the senses upon man's judgment is discussed at length in the "Apologie de Raimond Sebond"; however, the senses constantly harass man's ability to judge effectively, and Montaigne frequently refers to their debilitating capacity in other essays. Montaigne points out that one's judgment may be unhinged by the gnawing of a bone or by the scraping of a file. He adds that "les medecins tiennent qu'il y a certaines complexions qui s'agitent par aucuns sons et instrumens jusques à la fureur" (II, 12, 579). In all these examples sound is the culprit. A speaker's mellifluous voice is undoubtedly more persuasive than a harsh one. Caustic words lead to anger. It is interesting to note that these reactions are considered automatic and even instinctive, allowing little room for the thinking process usually associated with judgment. Hence, the faculty of judgment permeates the whole of one's psyche more than one would initially suspect; it is perhaps within many of these possibilities that one must see the indications that eventually lead Montaigne to substitute the all-inclusive term *vie* for *jugement* with relation to the notion of "essai." One can already distinguish these ambiguities in the proximity of the words *complexions*, properly rendered in English by temperaments, and *jugement*. Certainly, sensual reaction seems to be more a matter of temperament than of judgment.

GOD AND INSTITUTIONS

In the "Apologie de Raimond Sebond," Montaigne avowedly undertakes to defend Sebond's thesis that the truth of the Christian religion can be established "par raisons humaines et naturelles" (II, 12, 417). However, Montaigne soon reverses himself and mounts a colossal attack against the presumption of man. He argues that man does not possess knowledge and, furthermore, that he will never have it. Man is indeed a fool to think that by his own means he could ever know God or be anything other than what he is: "car il ne peut voir que de ses yeux, ny saisir que de ses prises. Il s'eslevera si Dieu lui preste extraordinairement la main" (II, 12, 588–589).

Throughout the essay, Montaigne utilizes his ingenuity to demolish reason as an intemperate, false, and presumptuous faculty which man takes to be his pride and joy:

J'appelle tousjours raison cette apparence de discours que chacun forge en soy; cette raison, de la condition de laquelle il y en peut avoir cent contraires autour d'un mesme subject, c'est un instrument de plomb et de cire, alongeable, ployable et accommodable à tous biais et à toutes mesures; il ne reste que la suffisance de le sçavoir contourner (II, 12, 548).

One can make of reason what one pleases. Montaigne attacks its unreliability and its inanity. As a means of acquiring knowledge, reason is an undependable asset; yet, it can be an asset. The faculty of reason described in the preceding quotation is but one side of the coin; certainly, this pejorative connotation prevails throughout the "Apologie de Raimond Sebond." The words *apparence, discours,* and *forge* emphasize the ephemeral and dubious nature of reason. More importantly, Montaigne is aware of the etymological sense of the term *discours*; it derives from Classical Latin *discursus*, Vulgar Latin *discurrere*, that is "courir çà et là, action de courir çà et là." [1] Although the meaning of "faculté, action de raisonner; raisonnement" [2] is a part of *discours*, the idea of "road," that is a zigzagging, irresponsible, dizzy pace, is frequently what Montaigne means. Montaigne castigates that reason which is merely discursive and theoretical and which beguiles man into thinking that it can solve metaphysical questions.

On the other hand, reason has a second meaning, for it implies a sensible, "natural" approach to things purely human; this form of reason is man's critical spirit. Reason can be equated with "nature"; that which is "natural" is likely to be reasonable. This "natural" reason can be an effective force in man's life and lead to happiness. In his discussion of Montaigne's skepticism, Jeanson remarks that "l'homme est capable d'un jugement droit sur le plan de la conduite, et Montaigne ne maintient sa condamnation qu'à l'égard de cette autre raison qui se veut explicative: c'est sur le plan de la connaissance théorique, et seulement sur ce plan, que son scepticisme demeure entier." [3] Hence, in human affairs, reason, or "jugement" as Jeanson calls it, can guide man. It has been noted earlier that the role of judgment is one of active guidance and prudence in the intellectual and moral conduct of man. It becomes apparent that Montaigne either equates judgment and reason, in the positive sense of the term, or that he places judgment above reason. Nevertheless, one must recall that judgment

[1] Oscar Bloch and W. von Wartburg, *Dictionnaire étymologique de la langue française* (Paris, 1960), p. 194.
[2] Pierre Villey in *Les Essais de Michel de Montaigne*, ed. Fortunat Strowski *et al.* (Bordeaux, 1906–1933), V, 212.
[3] Francis Jeanson, *Montaigne par lui-même* (Paris, 1951), p. 78.

can be an ineffectual tool and that perhaps Montaigne is equating it with bad reason when he berates its stupidity. [1]

It seems that judgment is superior to reason, and paradoxically this may be seen in the function which Montaigne ascribes to judgment when confronted with questions on the subject of God and religious and political institutions.

Montaigne recommends skepticism as a way of life because it paves the way to a greater awareness and acceptance of God:

> Il n'est rien en l'humaine invention où il y ait tant de verisimilitude et d'utilité. Cette-cy presente l'homme nud et vuide, recognoissant sa foiblesse naturelle, propre à recevoir d'en haut quelque force estrangere, desgarni d'humaine science, et d'autant plus apte à loger en soy la divine, aneantissant son jugement pour faire plus de place à la foy (II, 12, 486).

Pyrrhonism annihilates man's judgment; in other words, Montaigne recommends that man place blinders upon his judgment in order to know God. Because judgment is a human, natural faculty, it should attempt to reign in its own human territory; divine matters are not of its concern. As a faculty, judgment questions and seeks to establish relationships; but, where God is concerned, faith alone can make Him known, and unbridled inquisitiveness and reasoning are detrimental to a true knowledge of God:

> Le neud qui devroit attacher nostre jugement et nostre volonté, qui devroit estreindre nostre ame et joindre à nostre createur, ce devroit estre un neud prenant ses repliz et ses forces, non pas de noz considerations, de noz raisons et passions, mais d'une estreinte divine et supernaturelle, n'ayant qu'une forme, un visage et un lustre, qui est l'authorité de Dieu et sa grace (II, 12, 424).

Montaigne emphatically reiterates what was one of the most important points of his first objection to Sebond's detractors, namely that, even if knowlege of God were able to penetrate our souls by way of reason, it would in no way equal that obtained by faith alone. Wherever Montaigne advises judgment to remain within its territorial boundaries there is an implicit acceptance of the fact that whatever restraint

[1] Pierre Barrière, *Montaigne, gentilhomme français* (Paris, 1948), p. 162, argues that "pour bien comprendre Montaigne, comme au fond Descartes, il est nécessaire de ne pas confondre deux choses en apparence semblables; la raison qui s'égare dans sa présomption, et le bon sens, tout simple dans la conscience qu'il a de ses limites et de ses seules applications terrestres et pratiques." Needless to say, much confusion of terms exists. Barrière calls *bon sens* what Jeanson terms *jugement*. It is generally agreed that it is the pejorative meaning of reason which remains the butt of Montaigne's skepticism; unfortunately, there is no agreement as to whether *jugement*, *raison*, in the positive sense of the term, and *sens* are identical or whether they merely complement each other. Barrière's statement, for one, is misleading if not erroneous, since for Montaigne *sens*, as opposed to *jugement*, has no inkling of its shortcomings.

judgment can muster must come of its own accord. It is judgment itself which must define and ordain its limitations. It is not suggested that judgment could reason the articles of the Christian faith if it chose to try; rather, Montaigne sees the superiority of judgment over reason in its awareness of its weaknesses and in its voluntary recognition of those areas of knowledge with which it can deal effectively. One of the basic differences between reason and judgment seems to be Montaigne's assumption that reason *cannot* deal with God and that judgment *must not* attempt to do so. Reason and judgment are not alike; reason remains within the sphere of judgment and must be controlled and guided by it.

Humility and obedience, two qualities unknown to reason, enable man to better himself. Reason, the capacity to think discursively and make abstractions, has no knowledge of itself, and consequently, is unable to curb its activity. Judgment and reason are not mutually exclusive; on the contrary, they are interdependent. However, when judgment does not control reason, when it does not prescribe its paths, it fails to function properly :"il ne faut pas laisser au jugement de chacun la cognoissance de son devoir; il le lui faut prescrire, non pas le laisser choisir à son discours" (II, 12, 467). *Discours* or reason functions as an extension of judgment; its discourse provides the basis for judgment's knowledge. Hence, Montaigne is prone to admonish the more capable and responsible judgment. In the "Apologie de Raimond Sebond," Montaigne is not yet prepared to consider judgment as the one faculty which can mold man's life. Nevertheless, he appears to have seen possibilities in its wake which he refuses to attribute to reason.

There is a vigorous strain of skepticism in Montaigne which outlasts the years of the "Apologie." [1] When he reviews his text, he adds examples and elaborations that unfailingly emphasize his original thought. Although he places great faith in the ability of his judgment to steer a proper course throughout the trials of his intellectual and moral life, he never ceases to downgrade its performance in religion. Montaigne is a skeptic because of his acute faculty of judgment; but his skepticism does not impede his Catholicism, because he has willingly and forcefully forbidden his judgment to interfere in matters of religion. The following epitaph recognizes and illustrates the effortless ease with

[1] For an arresting and significant consideration of the "Apologie de Raimond Sebond" as an attack on rationalists, and particularly Calvinist rationalism, rather than a Pyrrhonist tract on universal doubt, see Floyd Gray, "The' nouveaux docteurs' and the Problem of Montaigne's Consistency in the *Apologie de Raymond Sebond*," *Symposium*, 18 (1964), 22–34.

which Montaigne was able to combine the two: "Moi qui à la doctrine chrétienne, ai allié la doctrine pyrrhonienne." [1]

In "De la coustume et de ne changer aisément une loy receüe," Montaigne attempts to expose the relativity of our learning and of the laws of reason. Accordingly, he shuns change, "car qui se mesle de choisir et de changer, usurpe l'authorité de juger, et se doit faire fort de voir la faute de ce qu'il chasse, et le bien de ce qu'il introduit" (I, 23, 120). Montaigne's political and religious conservatism rests upon a belief in a higher authority than man's, one which is beyond his control. His use of the term *usurpe* shows how strongly he feels. Even in the impetuousness of his early youth, he abstained from judging "ces grands corps," for he did not dare judge, "en sain jugement," matters of lesser importance in which rashness of judgment could do no harm. It is evident that the term *jugement* has a great deal to do with one's state of mind, and the type of judgment which Montaigne prefers is usually associated with the adjectives *sain* and *rassis*. When Montaigne pictures himself "en sain jugement," he sees a man whose state of mind is calm and free from agitation, in other words a man whom one might call level-headed. This state is opposed to rashness of judgment, or in French, "la temerité de juger." Montaigne deplores all departures from normality; all flutterings and unwarranted agitations of mind are an indication of poor judgment. Attempting to judge the higher institutions of man is an extreme action and beyond judgment's capacity to understand: "Toutes les voyes extravagantes me fachent" (II, 12, 541).

Montaigne unerringly visualizes the act of judgment as one in which one thing is accepted while another is rejected. In the preceding quotation, *choisir*, *changer*, and *juger* are intimately linked, and *changer* is perhaps the key idea. All things are characterized by motion, but change does not automatically ensue; change is wrought through the active acceptance and rejection of things, knowledge, and ideas which already exist. When Montaigne turns his judgment upon himself, it is for the purpose, not only of discovering himself, but also of changing that self, of improving it. Judgment is action, and it leads to action. Consequently, Montaigne wishes to restrict its activity in certain domains of knowledge. He does not see the act of judgment as one in which judgment merely catalogues the truth and falsehood, good and evil of new appearances; judgment must act upon its findings. It is for this reason that Montaigne fears the involvement of judgment in

[1] Cited in Armand Müller, *Montaigne* (Bruges, 1965), p. 28. However, there is no evidence to suggest that Montaigne composed his own epitaph; very probably he did not.

certain areas; judgment is incapable of grasping the import of the whole, and its acceptance and rejection of any of the parts is always unfounded and prone to obliterate the whole:

Il y a grand doute, s'il se peut trouver si evident profit au changement d'une loy receue, telle qu'elle soit, qu'il y a de mal à la remuer, d'autant qu'une police, c'est comme un bastiment de diverses pieces jointes ensemble, d'une telle liaison, qu'il est impossible d'en esbranler une que tout le corps ne s'en sente (I, 23, 117–118).

In the case of political and religious questions Montaigne remains particularly adamant in his condemnation of the use of judgment. After the successful publication of the first two books of his *Essais* in 1580, he set out to travel through France, Germany, and Italy. During this eighteen-month trip, he acquired a sense of belonging, of solidarity and unity with the human race, a feeling which was not prevalent prior to his departure, as the closing lines of "De la ressemblance des enfans aux peres" attest: "Et ne fut jamais au monde deux opinions pareilles, non plus que deux poils ou deux grains. Leur plus universelle qualité, c'est la diversité" (II, 37, 766). One of the significant aspects of his trip is the burgeoning of a simple and personal experimental method.[1] Montaigne develops a desire to confront experience. He is not content with hearsay; he wishes to see, to experience for himself. He used to judge mainly within the familiar surroundings of his tower; now he senses the need for experience.

By the time he returns to France, the interrelationship of judgment and experience has made its mark upon his thinking and his method of approach where the *Essais* are concerned.[2] In "Des boyteux," he recalls a village scene in which a young man and two associates proceeded to deceive the town by antics performed while hiding behind the church altar. One can imagine the number of people who were convinced that it was a miracle. However, exposure led to prison for the offenders, and Montaigne concludes:

On voit cler en cette cy, qui est descouverte; mais en plusieurs choses de pareille qualité, surpassant nostre connoissance, je suis d'advis que nous soustenons nostre jugement aussi bien à rejetter qu'à recevoir (III, 11, 1007).

There are manifestations that escape man's capacity to judge. A miracle or a fraud which masquerades as a miracle is not a proper test

[1] What might be considered an attempt to control experience by means of judgment is discussed in Chapter III.

[2] It is interesting to note the number of instances in which portions of Book III dwell at length on personal conversations, material details of all kinds, and short trips into the countryside. It might be worthwhile to study their effect upon the composition of an essay as opposed to the structural influence exerted by various readings.

of judgment; even a personal experience of this nature is bad preparation for a determination of truth and falsehood. Judgment must recognize that certain areas of experience exceed its ability to understand. It is on this plane that the famous and often misunderstood "Que sçay-je?" remains a constructive force for good.

THE EMOTIONAL NATURE OF MAN

The emotional nature of man frequently overpowers reason and judgment; a reconciliation must be effected and the advantage given to judgment. The ability to reason and the capacity to judge are of little avail to man if he proves unable to master his emotions and impress them in his service. When judgment succeeds in governing man's emotions, a powerful equilibrium is formed; man functions as a whole, unhampered in his activity by unwanted and uncontrollable impulses.

The relationship between judgment and feelings immediately summons up images of the Cornelian hero as an example of the supremacy of the former over the latter. However, it is noteworthy that for Corneille, as well as for Montaigne, judgment does not destroy passion; rather, it works through them so that they are made to be seen as extensions and manifestations of judgment. Although the Cornelian hero is an extreme example, too eager to envelop his extraordinary outbursts in the cloak of reason, the roots of this phenomenon can be found in Montaigne; as Armaingaud comments, Montaigne "ne condamne pas la passion, il en demande seulement le contrôle." [1]

Control, or the verb *régler*, as noted earlier, is a key term in Montaigne's concept of judgment. Emotional disturbances cannot be easily eradicated; moreover, they can be forces for positive action if they are mastered. Montaigne argues that man is a mass of divergent impulses which create a lack of balance within the human psyche. Control of these stimulants produces mental and moral excellence; on the other hand, when they prove to be stronger than judgment, the result is a diseased mind.

It is difficult to ascertain whether judgment or another area of the psyche is the center of all emotions; however, emotional upheaval caused by love, fear, anger, and other intense sentiments is so uniformly

[1] Arthur Armaingaud, ed. *Œuvres complètes de Michel de Montaigne* (Paris, 1924–1941), IV, 26, n. 1.

presented as the result of a distorted judgment that it is reasonable to assume that *jugement* frequently refers to emotional composure and the total psyche (*âme* and *esprit*). The difference in meaning is striking if one recalls Montaigne's description of judgment in "De Democritus et Heraclitus" in which he, the "je" of the passage, utilizes as he sees fit the ability or faculty of judgment, "un util à tous subjects."

Confusion of the terms *esprit* and *jugement* is unavoidable, and one of the reasons is found in Montaigne's use of Latin quotations. When speaking of man's vulnerability to psychological change, Montaigne refers to Cicero's translation of two lines from the Odyssey: "Tales sunt hominum mentes, quali pater ipse/Juppiter auctifera lustravit lampade terras." [1] The Latin *mens* and the French *esprit* of Thibaudet's translation are all-inclusive terms; the human organism is divided into matter and mind, *mens*. Immediately following the Latin quotation, Montaigne uses the term *jugement* in his continuing analysis of the psychological "branle":

> Ce ne sont pas seulement les fievres, les breuvages et les grands accidens qui renversent nostre jugement; les moindres choses du monde le tournevirent (II, 12, 547).

The proximity of *mens* and *jugement* suggests a significant equation: judgment implies the mind in general. In order that the mind not be taken to mean strictly intellectual activity, it can be said that *jugement* frequently represents total psychological life as opposed to the physical body. Hence, it is perhaps best to describe judgment as an intellectual, moral, and emotional faculty. It is the part of man which continually registers and reacts to all change, physical and psychological:

> à peine se peut il rencontrer une seule heure en la vie où nostre jugement se trouve en sa deuë assiete, nostre corps estant subject à tant de continuelles mutations, et estofé de tant de sortes de ressorts (II, 12, 548).

In a passage of the "Apologie" suppressed after 1588, Montaigne maintains that emotions produce perpetual mutations in the soul and that it is constantly subject to their tyranny. Moreover, he asks: "Le jugement d'un homme courroucé, ou de celuy qui est en crainte, est-ce le jugement qu'il aura tantost quand il sera rassis" (II, 12, 551)? It is probable that Montaigne omitted the statement in the course of his post-1588 revisions because he had previously expressed this thought in the "Apologie." This suppression also suggests an augmentation of Montaigne's faith in the powers of judgment. Nevertheless, the sentence

[1] Trans. Thibaudet: "L'esprit humain changeant ressemble sur la terre / Au mobile rayon dont le dieu la féconde."

stressed the instability of judgment and, as a separate faculty of the psyche, its subservience to man's changing moods and temperament. The composition of the quoted lines indicates the lack of control which judgment exercises upon the remainder of the psyche; in fact, judgment is placed in a passive role; instead of remaining an active force, it becomes a helpless recipient. Its inability to sense and to know the change taking place within itself stems from the fact that *jugement* represents not the faculty of judgment, or at least not exclusively, but mental outlook, state, or attitude.

Montaigne is fully cognizant of the importance of the imponderables of psychic life. Man is beset by differing moods and feelings which come and go at random and whose motives he can neither detect nor explain. Montaigne's awareness of the dark reaches of man's subconscious affects his probes of the psyche. He does not label that area of psychic life; he is conscious of its existence and of the influence which it exerts upon the psychological conscience of man.[1] He seeks to fathom the portent of subconscious activity within himself, but he usually despairs of attaining any degree of success:

> Maintenant je suis à tout faire, maintenant à rien faire; ce qui m'est plaisir à cette heure, me sera quelque fois peine. Il se faict mille agitations indiscretes et casuelles chez moy. Ou l'humeur melancholique me tient, ou la cholerique; et de son authorité privée à cet'heure le chagrin prédomine en moy, à cet'heure l'alegresse (II, 12, 549).

This passage was added to the 1582 edition of the *Essais*; however, the adjectives "indiscretes et casuelles" are a post-1588 correction; the 1582 phrase which was replaced read "sans le congé du jugement." Initially, Montaigne seems to place the blame on judgment: he feels that it is the role of judgment to master those unfathomable impulses. He is troubled by the instability of his moods, feelings, and desires. The post-1588 suppression of "sans le congé du jugement" suggests Montaigne's increasing faith in the power of judgment. The terms "indiscretes et casuelles" place greater emphasis on the portent and complexity of psychic life but, at the same time, they release judgment from responsibility for the unpredictability of subconscious states of being.

He recognizes a vast difference between the conscious and subconscious areas of the psyche. He does not know the exact relation of

[1] F. J. Billeskov Jansen, in his perceptive study of Montaigne's personality, remarks that "le philosophe a ouvert des vues intéressantes et fécondes sur le caractère multiple et malléable de notre esprit: il ne nous a pas décrit dans une démonstration méthodique, la nature particulière et l'importance respective de chacun des éléments psychiques," pp. 46-47.

one to the other, yet control of the subconscious strikes him as an activity of judgment. Montaigne does not bewail the fact that he is happy at times and sad at others; perhaps he would enjoy ordering himself to be sad or happy, as his judgment might dictate. Whatever psychic manifestation judgment might approve would in no way determine the intellectual or moral validity of those manifestations. Hence, the meaning which Montaigne attaches to the faculty of judgment in this example (II, 12, 549) is truly, in the most modern connotation, a psychological one. Judgment is not asked to rule on the truth or falsehood, good or evil, of Montaigne's varying frames of mind; it is asked to fathom these psychological disturbances and control them. Montaigne recognizes the "authorité privée" of the subconscious, an authority which he would like to circumvent by means of judgment. The purely psychological role of judgment, as opposed to its intellectual and moral functions, tends to equate judgment with the will [1] and more specifically with psychological conscience as opposed to the subconscious.

There are three motives which consistently appear throughout the *Essais* as obstacles to judgment: love, fear, and anger.[2] Judgment is quick to succumb to love and desire. As Montaigne remarks, those who attempt to arrest the progress of concupiscence promptly realize "la force de cette conversion et alteration que nostre jugement souffre" (II, 12, 552). Montaigne has tried to control his appetite; he succeeds only in acutely witnessing the progressive feebleness of his resistance: "l'image des choses me commençoit à paroistre autre que de coustume." Conversely, as his craving diminishes, he sees his soul "reprendre une autre sorte de veuë, autre estat et autre jugement." This last *jugement* refers to the result achieved by the former *jugement*, that is the faculty of judgment. In other words, his judgment or his appreciation of the situation changes with the passing of his desire. The significance of this relationship is that judgment is completely bypassed by passion. Judgment is deceived by cupidity and, more importantly, it deceives

[1] While in the throes of passion, judgment is unable to establish the good or evil of desire because Montaigne does not seem to ask it to do so. His only concern is the amount of control that judgment can exert upon desire. When he says, "j'ay autrefois entrepris de me tenir bandé pour la passion soustenir et rabatre" (II, 12, 552), the directing "je," in its actions of "entreprendre," "tenir bandé," "soustenir," and "rabatre," presents itself as *volonté* or will power. There are times when it is a question of imposition of will, for the activity of judgment does not always imply the strict determination of truth from falsehood, good from evil.

[2] Most of the limitations which affect judgment are noted in the "Apologie de Raimond Sebond"; although Montaigne does not deny them elsewhere, it is difficult to ascertain how thoroughly he confirms them all elsewhere in the *Essais*.

itself willfully. Judgment can be pitiably blind to reality and subservient to physical appearances, as the following lines demonstrate:

Je ne puis dire assez souvant combien j'estime la beauté qualité puissante et advantageuse.... Elle tient le premier rang au commerce des hommes; elle se presente au devant, seduict et preoccupe nostre jugement avec grande authorité et merveilleuse impression (III, 12, 1035).

When Montaigne refers to the conversion and alteration of judgment wrought by passion, one wonders why he chooses judgment as the faculty which experiences the disorder. He usually associates judgment with the intellectual and moral aspects of life. Montaigne does not condemn passion on moral grounds; the covetousness of which he speaks eludes morality because it is a physical phenomenon. It exists as an advancing and receding uncontrollable impulse which has little association with the normal concerns of judgment. In fact, imagination is a powerful force in such circumstances, and Montaigne recognizes the importance of its activity. He argues that, once the "chaleur du desir" has left him, the perceptions of his judgment are no longer the same. While stimulated by passion, he perceives no difficulties in the path of his undertaking; indeed, his *discours* and his conscience recede into the background. When desire leaves him, he notices only difficulties. His interest lies in the truth or falsehood of his judgment's evaluation of the obstructions or lack of them: "Lequel plus veritablement" (II, 12, 552)? Conscience is entirely distinct from judgment in this example. The judgment which undergoes change is different from the one which is unable to distinguish the true impression. If judgment is altered, its evaluation of two propositions can only be false; moreover, that which is non-existent or annihilated cannot render judgment. There seems to be a confusion of roles and abilities due to the complex nature of the psyche.

Fear is often discussed by Montaigne in conjunction with judgment. In fact, in the first years of his writing, he devoted a short essay to it, "De la peur." For Montaigne, the faculty which senses fear, which is most stricken and affected by it, is judgment:

Je ne suis pas bon naturaliste (qu'ils disent) et ne sçay guiere par quels ressors la peur agit en nous; mais tant y a que c'est une estrange passion; et disent les medecins qu'il n'en est aucune qui emporte plustost nostre jugement hors de sa deuë assiette. De vray, j'ay veu beaucoup de gens devenus insensez de peur (I, 18, 74).

As he remarks, it drives some people to insanity. It has already been observed that the loss of judgment can be equated with insanity. For such occurrences, Montaigne's vocabulary and imagery are fairly consistent; it is a matter of judgment being "emporté ... hors de sa deuë assiette" or "de son siege." Whatever the cause of fear, it renders man irrational. Judgment has no control over it; for that matter, judgment is not responsible for its inception because no thought processes are involved. Undoubtedly, if one is driven out of one's wits by fear, one is unable to function properly mentally. Certainly, one would be unable to judge the import of an impending catastrophe, given that the feeling of approaching disaster, for example, would have originated the phenomenon of fear which obliterates judgment. The verb *to obliterate* summarizes the impact of fear upon judgment; it effaces judgment completely; more importantly, what it extinguishes is not the ability to judge; rather, it is the capacity to receive any other impression, to think.

There is a major difference between a diseased mind and one which is deranged; the former still functions while the latter is suspended. In those instances in which Montaigne refers to judgment in connection with the emotion of fear, he is not attributing to judgment the limited scope of one faculty among many. On the contrary, judgment represents all conscious and rational psychic life, for it incorporates all the other faculties.

In "De l'yvrongnerie," Montaigne extends his indictment of fear to drunkenness, which, to his mind, "entre les autres, me semble un vice grossier et brutal.... Les autres vices alterent l'entendement: cettuy-cy le renverse, et estonne le corps" (II, 2, 322). If one equates *entendement* and *jugement* in this example, one confronts the major distinction to be made between various emotions and vices which constantly harass judgment; although some alter judgment, it continues to function, however crippled it may be; others, and they are neither worse nor better, for Montaigne uses the terms *renverser* and *emporter hors* indiscriminately, completely overwhelm it:

> Pensent ils qu'une Apoplexie n'estourdisse aussi bien Socrates qu'un portefaix? Les uns ont oublié leur nom mesme par la force d'une maladie, et une legiere blessure a renversé le jugement à d'autres (II, 12, 328).

All aberrations and deviations, whether of psychological or physical provenience, affect the faculty of judgment. The verbs *estourdir*, *oublier*, and *renverser* equally refer to judgment; it is Socrates' judgment which is stunned by apoplexy; temporary amnesia is due to a loss of judgment and shock or the overturning of one's judgment is the result of a wound. In each case, as he did in that of La Boétie, Montaigne implies consciousness or the awareness of what is happening around one. In these occurrences, judgment represents the total mind.

Pain and fear are linked to another connotation of judgment in "Que philosopher, c'est apprendre a mourir." The "vulgaire" prefer not to think of death; mere mention of it makes them hastily cross themselves. They dislike to write wills because they associate them with death. They procrastinate until the very end, "et Dieu sçait lors, entre la douleur et la frayeur, de quel bon jugement ils vous le patissent" (I, 20, 82).

If *jugement* refers to the faculty, Montaigne is implying that this faculty is unable to draw up a will equitably; in other words, fear renders the "vulgaire" unreasonable and incapable of correctly distributing their property. However, a different interpretation of the statement is more likely. In fact, Montaigne's irony seems to indicate that *jugement* is neither a faculty nor a quality in this example; it is an apprehensive attitude which refers to the legator's frame of mind. The verb *pâtir* adds to this possibility; in effect, Montaigne is saying: With what "graciousness" they submit to its ordeal!

The third major emotion, anger, is highly destructive; it alters the person who is affected by its vehemence, and it often leads to regrettable action: "Il n'est passion qui esbranle tant la sincerité des jugemens que la colere" (II, 31, 692). Although *jugemens* could be either the faculty or the act of judgment, it is more likely that the acts of judgment are in question in this case. Montaigne speaks from long experience as a counselor in the Chambre des Enquêtes of the Parlement de Bordeaux. Accordingly, he uses judges and their courts when discussing the influence of anger upon judgment; in these occurrences, judgment is so impaired as to be incapable of adjusting the punishment to the crime. In the "Apologie," Montaigne decries the ease with which sentences can differ day by day and case to case as a result of nefarious influences upon the individual judgment:

> Tel qui raporte de sa maison la douleur de la goute, la jalousie, ou le larrecin de son valet, ayant toute l'ame teinte et abreuvée de colere, il ne faut pas douter que son jugement ne s'en altere vers cette part là (II, 12, 547).

No doubt, the judgment which finds itself hindered by sickness and anger cannot see things as they are; its perception follows the course of distortion; appearances are true or false before judgment can determine the difference. "Pente" and "inclination" instantly propel judgment in one direction. Nevertheless, judgment's usual intellectual function is not the only meaning associated with the *jugement* of this passage. Judgment is identified with mood and more importantly with emotional composure. In fact, all the impulsions discussed in this chapter are emotionally based in their relation to judgment, and their effect is described in terms of psychological imbalance.

The psychological complexities which confront judgment do not alter its intellectual connotation. Anger and fear may elicit various responses from judgment and thereby lead to differing interpretations; however, the basic role of judgment is to think rationally and well. Montaigne states that in discussions one should not be angered by contradictions, for the participants seek the same end:

La cause de la verité devroit estre la cause commune à l'un et à l'autre. Que respondra-il? la passion du courroux luy a desjà frappé le jugement. Le trouble s'en est saisi avant la raison (III, 8, 902).

This example demonstrates that judgment has the capacity to think well in the search for truth and that anger disturbs this ability.

It was noted earlier in this study that a viable balance must be established between emotions or man's nature and his judgment. Whether judgment is an intellectual and moral faculty of the psyche or whether it represents the entire psyche, psychological conscience, or consciousness, tenacious sentiment always effects a decrease in its power of centralization and control. As Montaigne implies in the following lines, the role of judgment is the accumulation of knowledge, an asset which is of little value if judgment cannot exercise self-control:

Si nostre jugement est en main à la maladie mesmes et à la perturbation; si c'est de la folie et de la temerité qu'il est tenu de recevoir l'impression des choses, quelle seurté pouvons nous attendre de luy (II, 12, 551)?

Too often judgment is prone to relinquish its beneficent and restraining effect upon the disparate elements which form man. Judgment must control man; it need not always countermand nature; rather, it is to work with nature. Coexistence is not only possible but inevitable; hence, an equilibrium must be attained whereby both judgment and nature are satisfied. Montaigne consistently insists that judgment examine all natural and instinctive actions and reactions in order that the individual be at peace with himself. Man cannot master his actions until he can rationalize his nature.

DEFICIENCY: A PRACTICAL GUIDE

Authentic judgment knows that it errs and that it is subject to its own interest and aspirations to authoritativeness. The difficulty of maintaining propitious harmony is attested by the numerous transgressions of judgment. Throughout Montaigne's work, there are numerous pejorative descriptions of judgment which escape the categories previously established in this chapter. In general, inadequacies and foolish actions on the part of judgment are linked to its diversity and instability; judgment frequently contradicts itself, and it is constrained by habit and custom. Montaigne criticizes the performance of judgment during the successive periods of his composition. Although his faith in the capabilities of judgment increases, he continues to indict it in his textual revisions by the addition of pejorative remarks. The examples studied in this section substantiate Hill Hay's statement that "diversité, contradiction, instabilité, voilà les mots qui se présentent à son esprit quand il examine le jugement de l'homme." [1] However, this harsh appraisal needs to be modified in the light of Montaigne's increasing dependence and reliance on judgment.

In "De l'inequalité qui est entre nous," Montaigne concludes that the difference between two men is greater than that between a given man and an animal. Infinite diversity best describes the human condition. However, for example, the fact that some men are Kings and others subjects does not constitute a "dissemblance essentielle" (I, 42, 252). Moreover, those who would gladly assume command, a role "qui semble estre si doux" (I, 42, 255), are not only unaware of the true nature of diversity, but they are also foolish, for Montaigne thinks that it is easier to follow in the footsteps of others and obey their directives than to guide and command, "considerant l'imbecillité du jugement humain et la difficulté du chois és choses nouvelles et doubteuses" (I, 42, 255). Although this remark is highly critical of judgment's abilities, it is a concise summation of the intellectual role which Montaigne assigns to the faculty of judgment.

Montaigne is aware of the weakness of judgment and the difficulty of its task. Judgment is not deemed weak because of its difficulties; rather, the two are complementary. Montaigne recognizes an inherent weakness in the structure of judgment; no other faculty or superior force is equipped to legitimize and authenticate judgment's reasoning; this is the lesson of "De l'incertitude de nostre jugement." Judgment

[1] Hill Hay, p. 131.

can reason in favor of a matter as well as it can against it, but the outcome, that is the truth or falsehood of its choice, can be seen only in the events which follow judgment's pronouncement.

In the "Apologie," Montaigne demonstrates that the immense diversity of opinions which man encounters in life rests upon the "divers lustres et diverses considerations" generated by the subjects under discussion. No two objects or topics are perceived in the same way by any two individuals. It is a notion which he expresses again forcefully in "De l'experience":

> Jamais deux hommes ne jugerent pareillement de mesme chose, et est impossible de voir deux opinions semblables exactement, non seulement en divers hommes, mais en mesme homme à diverses heures (III, 13, 1044).

Reason can render opposite actions plausible. The essay "De l'incertitude de nostre jugement" maintains the same thesis; however, the term *jugement* appears only in the title. The list of contradictory possibilities is attributed to the faculty of *discours*, which is usually, but not always, synonymous with *raison*. The faculty of *raison* as such is not mentioned in the essay. The condition of *jugement* in "De l'incertitude de nostre jugement" is analogous to that of *raison* in the following passage: "la raison fournit d'apparence à divers effects. C'est un pot à deux ances, qu'on peut saisir à gauche et à dextre" (II, 12, 565–566). Both *raison* (II, 12) and *jugement* (I, 47) are presented as the faculties which attempt to establish the plausibility of various incidents and ideas. Montaigne makes no detectable distinction between these occurrences of *raison* and *jugement*; they are identical. Moreover, the editions of 1580 and 1582 contained after the word *effects* a redundant sentence in which the shortcomings of reason were also attributed to judgment: "Il advient de céte diversité de visages que les jugemens s'appliquent diversement au chois des choses." It could be argued that reason discourses upon phenomena, while judgment makes the final evaluation by choosing and deciding: in effect, reason and judgment are frequently seen to complement each other in this manner. Nevertheless, the juxtaposition of *raison* and *jugement* in the expression of certain ideas indicates that they can be synonymous, not only in terms of the positive sense of *raison*, but also in relation to logical, but unproved thinking.

Judgment encounters great difficulty in the course of its activity; it has no guarantee that its choice is the correct one. As previously noted, some judgments are never able to evaluate properly, at least in certain matters; the instinctive and emotional properties of certain human beings are unmanageable. Judgment is also a weak faculty because of its unreasonable attitude in the face of intricate frivolities:

C'est un tesmoignage merveilleux de la foiblesse de nostre jugement, qu'il recommande les choses par la rareté ou nouvelleté, ou encore par la difficulté, si la bonté et utilité n'y sont joinctes (I, 54, 298).

Judgment allows itself to be moved by "vaines subtilitez"; the inability to assign the proper degree of functional worth to various activities constitutes a lack of judgment. Judgment is frequently irresponsible; it acts unadvisedly, and it is too uncritically receptive. In "Des loix somptuaires," Montaigne refers to Plato's injunctions against the irresponsible freedom which youth, "remuant son jugement tantost en cette assiette, tantost en cette là, courant après les nouvelletez, honorant leurs inventeurs" (I, 43, 261), claims as its prerogative. Youth's judgment or inquisitive power knows no restraint; it has not yet learned to proceed with caution, to perceive and inquire without automatically accepting and changing. Montaigne stresses the idea that judgment must neither approve nor condemn various actions until it has closely examined them.

Judgment is the seat of one's opinions vis-à-vis all of life. However, it is in this capacity that it proves to be most unstable. Man's opinions or judgments comprise a series of contradictions. One will reject tomorrow what one believes today:

ne m'est-il pas advenu, non une fois, mais cent, mais mille, et tous les jours, d'avoir ambrassé quelqu'autre chose à tout ces mesmes instrumens, en cette mesme condition, que depuis j'aye jugée fauce (II, 12, 546)?

Yet judgment remains the best storehouse of man's total experience, for it is on the basis of accumulated knowledge that man formulates his opinions.

Montaigne's often-quoted phrase "au moins faut il devenir sage à ses propres despans," which immediately follows the preceding quotation, has elicited much commentary and is generally considered one of the key phrases to an understanding of his unpretentious and practical philosophy of nature. This thought expresses Montaigne's notion that not only judgments but also life imply contradiction. Lack of judgment in the present is perhaps due to a lack of experience; more importantly, the opinion which changes today will of necessity change tomorrow or the next day as new experiences transform judgment's capacity to judge. Knowledge is relative and anchored in experience; to become wiser at one's expense implies a belief in the inevitability of varying judgments. Every gain in the realm of knowledge and in the search for wisdom is accompanied by a corresponding loss of an idea or theory maintained earlier. The phrase represents an undeclared insight into the properties of judgment which eventually leads to Montaigne's increased faith in judgment's capacity to orient man throughout life.

Like imagination, judgment can be a deceiving power: "Qui se souvient de s'estre tant et tant de fois mesconté de son propre jugement, est-il pas un sot de n'en entrer pour jamais en deffiance" (III, 13, 1051)? Judgment bears scrutiny; no matter how responsible it may have proved itself to be, there will always be occasions when another man's reasoning will demonstrate that one was championing a false opinion. It is interesting to note that Montaigne wrote these lines in 1587–1588, long after he had fused the faculty of judgment and the self into the only tool worthwhile for the discovery of knowledge. In this example and several others, one observes Montaigne's constant awareness of the frailty of human judgment. However, recognition ("Qui se souvient") of one's mistaken opinions and reasonings is an effect of judgment to be prized above all others. Constantly confronted by choice, even the most experienced and best intentioned of judgments is bound to advocate some unjust cause, fail to perceive the significant aspects of an action, or misinterpret the appropriate facts. Man's judgment, or what Montaigne sometimes calls his "yeux internes" (I, 49, 285), as opposed to his sensory means of obtaining, judging, and classifying experience, can tire and become inoperative, miscalculate, or temporarily lose its power to compare effectively and decide correctly: "Il n'est jugement humain, si tendu, qui ne sommeille par fois" (II, 12, 525).

Lack of exercise and inexperience account for much of judgment's foolish actions and choices. The essay "Des coustumes anciennes" is devoted to the presentation of different and conflicting customs "afin qu'ayant en l'imagination cette continuelle variation des choses humaines, nous en ayons le jugement plus esclaircy et plus ferme" (I, 49, 285). Reflection upon this incessant variation decreases one's adherence to the absolute merits of one custom, action, or idea as against another.[1] Judgment is better equipped to compare appearances and make its de-

[1] In the same vein, in "De l'institution des enfans," Montaigne speaks of the knowledge which judgment obtains of its relativity when it is exposed to diversity: "Tant d'humeurs, de sectes, de jugemens, d'opinions, de loix et de coustumes nous apprennent à juger sainement des nostres, et apprennent nostre jugement à reconnoistre son imperfection et sa naturelle foiblesse" (I, 26, 157).

cision if it is not stunted by habit and tied to the attitudes and beliefs given to it by its birthplace, as Montaigne states elsewhere.[1] A certain dullness of intellect is born of inactivity and lack of exposure: "L'assuefaction endort la veuë de nostre jugement" (I, 23, 110). The faculty of judgment must pierce through habit in order to broaden its capacities and increase its ability to perceive truth. Consequently, motion, change, and diversity are necessary ingredients of judgment.

The follies, inconstancies, and inabilities of judgment inevitably rouse Montaigne's anger.[2] However, there is one infraction of judgment which is even more serious because its effect is more damaging to its own abilities and to man in general; it is judgment's almost total inability to divorce itself from subjective involvement with what appears before it for consideration. Montaigne refers to two historians who debate the relationship of king and subject; he notes that one denigrates the king's position while the other places him above God. Understandably, the first one is a democrat and the second a monarchist:

> Il est peu de choses ausquelles nous puissions donner le jugement syncere, parce qu'il en est peu ausquelles, en quelque façon, nous n'ayons particulier interest (III, 7, 896).

In the "Apologie," Montaigne insists that old age cannot be called upon to discuss its own relative merits because it is involved; [3] in order to judge objectively, one must be at once removed from and yet conversant with the object of investigation. It is for this reason that Montaigne endows the faculty of judgment with the ability to know itself and retract what it has formerly held.

Montaigne is acutely aware of the impact of man's physical nature upon judgment. Judgment is intimately associated with the corporeal presence of man, and the health or illness of either has a corresponding state in the other. Moreover, judgment is not always at liberty to control the myriad fluctuations within the somatic state of being. Inasmuch as incidents of all types can occur without its consent, the psychological control of judgment over body and psyche is greatly diminished. Only with advanced knowledge and control of itself can judgment hope to obtain and maintain a healthy equilibrium.

[1] I, 49, 284–285.

[2] III, 9, 958.

[3] II, 12, 585. The same idea is expressed in relation to judges in II, 12, 548. A slight variation is found in "Des livres," in which Montaigne states that Seneca's condemnation of Caesar's murderers is a concession to the tyranny of the emperors of his time. In other words, Seneca finds it expedient to do so: "c'est d'un jugement forcé qu'il condamne la cause de ces genereux meurtriers de Caesar" (II, 10, 393).

Man must proceed through life with caution and moderation. Falsehood is everywhere; everything is open to interpretation. The senses can easily deceive the soul, and the soul repays them in kind. Knowledge of man's physical state is immensely difficult because the body acts upon and reacts to itself and the soul: "Il est certain que nostre apprehension, nostre jugement et les facultez de nostre ame en general souffrent selon les mouvemens et alterations du corps, lesquelles alterations sont continuelles" (II, 12, 547). The body and judgment are in a constant state of flux, and the reaction of man's corporeal nature to change determines the mental health of the individual and the knowledge which judgment can have of physical and psychological phenomena. This does not imply that Montaigne accuses judgment of helplessness; on the contrary, he counsels judgment to be cautious in its search for knowledge, for it is an imperfect instrument. Although judgment is the best available tool, only awareness of its limitations will spare it grief and turmoil. Gauging the alterations of the body and the corresponding states which they produce within judgment and adjusting judgment accordingly so that its readings will better enable it to fathom not only the self, but the whole man, are of prime importance since man, if he is to have any knowledge of the world about him, must first know himself. Indeed, what one might call the physical, as opposed to psychological, limitations of judgment appear as an almost necessary apprenticeship of trial and error;[1] though frequently misleading, soundings of the body keep judgment aware of its deficiencies and make it a more alert and accurate instrument.

Close examination of the cases in which the effectiveness of the faculty of judgment is minimized and ridiculed reveals that Montaigne's invective is severest in the "Apologie de Raimond Sebond"; in fact, all the faculties of the mind and the uses which man makes of them are questioned in the "Apologie." The faculty of judgment continues to attract Montaigne's critical analysis throughout the *Essais* because he considers its functions to be most crucial for the progress of man. As he increasingly associates it with the search for knowledge through man himself, he comes to identify it with man's personality. Hence, in "De la vanité," he finds it possible to see major differences between his qualities and those demonstrated by the *jugements* of his day.[3]

[1] The physical aspect of judgment is discussed in greater detail in Chapter III, "Judgment and Being."

[2] III, 9, 958.

As the structure of judgment becomes more complex and organic because of its many associations with body and spirit, it is evident that its deficiencies as a faculty in the acquisition of true knowledge and its susceptibility to shortsightedness and error remain a matter of constant concern to Montaigne. When an increasing faith in the possibilities of judgment is coupled with a lingering awareness of its weakness, the formulation of a positive and "creative" educational program results. In time, enlightened judgment becomes one with its object; judgment becomes the innermost self.

CHAPTER III

JUDGMENT AND BEING

"The proper study of mankind is man"
Alexander Pope

Throughout the *Essais,* Montaigne treats the subject of thinking well on two levels, that is for Montaigne in particular and for man in general. As he looks about him and at history, he sees bad habits of thought linked to moral degeneracy. Consequently, he conceives of judgment as an intellectual and moral faculty, an instrument that can correct man's cognitive and moral deficiencies. Montaigne has witnessed its efficiency and capability within himself; self-trial, not antiquated principles of authority, is the touchstone of his mounting confidence in his ability to think correctly and recognize relative truths.

Montaigne's awareness of man's cognitive limitations leads him to delve deeply into his own being. He surmises that the complex of emotions and thoughts recognized as Michel de Montaigne is not only the closest test at hand of knowledge, but also the only one with which he is conversant on a daily and intimate level. If there is true knowledge, it must be the knowledge of being. If man becomes conscious of himself, if he studies, knows, and experiences himself, it is possible for him to apply this knowledge to other men and to other facets of life. Indeed, one man, Montaigne, may be the prism through which one can perceive humanity. Moreover, if his assumption proves false, his endeavor will be no less valuable, for, at the very least, Montaigne will know more about his own being, and his happiness will increase proportionately. The goal of self-knowledge is personal happiness.

Man is limited by his nature, by art, by habit, by custom, and particularly by presumption. In the "Apologie," Montaigne strives to reduce man's image of himself. Although Montaigne concludes that man can rise above himself and humanity only with the help of God, one also senses that Montaigne believes that it can be done if man is willing to be himself, and all that his nature entails, a man and nothing more. Being a man must be the measure of his sight, and being a man implies first of all being oneself. A strong sense of independence informs

Montaigne's formulation of the principles which constitute man's education and lead to his individual identity.

The pedagogical program which Montaigne enunciates in "Du pedantisme" and "De l'institution des enfans" stresses the formation of judgment because individual judgment is the seat of man's moral and intellectual independence. Montaigne's emerging belief in the value of self-observation and his examination of man's mental faculties in their relation to the acquisition of knowledge and truth lead him to the discovery that all psychic and moral problems must be resolved within the self, within oneself. The test of man's knowledge and moral worth becomes the ability to "judge" oneself. Intellectually and morally, man is obligated to deny the principle of authority; he must learn to view everything in terms of self.

Having shown at length in "Du pedantisme" and "De l'institution des enfans" the necessity of good thinking and the means to acquire a constant habit of reflection, Montaigne now perceives that intellectual and moral reflection as a method of correctly discerning the truth or falsehood, good or evil of appearances is also conducive to self-creation. If man turns his judgment inward, he will not only discover himself momentarily but also give himself being, permanent being in time and space. Hence, self-study incorporates the creation of a psychological identity which the observer of self can recognize, emulate, and portray. The faculty of judgment embodies man's psychological identity. However, judgment is also the observer. Consequently, judgment ultimately evokes both the "je" and the "moi" of Montaigne. This condition of Montaigne's psychic being is particularly noticeable in his contention that his *Essais* are the trials of his judgment.[1]

The complete import of Montaigne's notion of judgment emerges in the study of self. To some degree, it can be said that Montaigne progresses from theory to practice. In the "Apologie," he inquires into the efficacy of mental activity; he studies man's faculties in terms of what they are unable to do. On the other hand, in "De l'institution des enfans," he delineates man's possibilities; a properly trained judgment is man's guide to sound intellectual and moral achievements. Secure in the knowledge that the soundness of his judgment is his greatest attribute, Montaigne has yet to practice or test the reliability of his advice. He thinks and reasons about knowledge and morality; he must now experience them, that is observe and almost physically feel them

[1] I, 50, 289. The significance and evolution of this notion is studied in the last section of this chapter.

within himself. As he frequently remarks, *toucher au-dedans* becomes judgment's most important task.

Montaigne takes great pride in what he correctly senses to be the singular power of his judgment. As has already been noted in this study,[1] judgment and observation are intimately linked, and Montaigne possesses the gift of observation to an unusually high degree. In fact, observation and examination of all psychic and moral phenomena is a compulsive act on Montaigne's part. His insatiable curiosity and the enlightening experience afforded him by the appraisal of reason in the "Apologie" induce him to direct his innate judicious ability at himself and through him at man in general. The reality of his inner being, as it may be "judged" to be, is the most positive realm of truth and the only one which can lead to other essential truths. Montaigne's inner being becomes the object of his constant surveillance, and he entrusts the interpretation of self to the faculty of judgment, the only faculty which, because of its organic structure, can constantly keep abreast of the self and experience it as it emerges. Indeed, its emergence is due to the efforts of judgment. Judgment and self fuse into a psychically viable and palpable being.

With few exceptions, the majority of the *Essais* published in 1580 are not concerned with self-study. The relationship of judgment and self as the sole subject of the *Essais* emerges in Book III. At the outset of his literary career, Montaigne tends to conceive of his judgment as strictly an intellectual faculty. His judgment is outside of himself; it is directed outward, to other things, to other people. It is an intellectual aid which he can manipulate as he pleases.[2]

In the earliest essays, Montaigne's notion of judgment is simple and straightforward. He is not at all certain of his literary endeavor, although he does know that his capacity to judge is as good as that of his sources. Consequently, the first essays consist of Montaigne's personal opinions on a multitude of subjects. For him, to judge still means to pass judgment, to criticize and evaluate ideas, actions, and men. He enjoys confronting his judgment with that of others in order to measure his personal capacity. He frequently takes issue with his sources, for he evaluates the independent pertinency of his judgment by its ability to discern more than his predecessors.[3]

[1] See Chapter I, p. 27.

[2] I, 50, "De Democritus et Heraclitus," and, in this study, Chapter I, pp. 21–22.

[3] A good example is found in II, 4, "A demain les affaires." The Emperor sent a parcel to Rusticus, who was attending one of Plutarch's lectures on the evil of uncontrollable curiosity. Plutarch praises Rusticus for his composure and courtesy in not opening the parcel until the

The topics which Montaigne finds most interesting are political history, human nature, pain, and death.[1] For the most part, these subjects are primarily responsible for the moral outlook which gradually permeates the faculty of judgment. Montaigne discriminates and judges intellectually among a number of actions and ideas. However, his judgment normally perceives the relative degree of good or evil of the action because Montaigne is interested in its significance for himself. Montaigne fears pain and death and seeks to renew within himself the wisdom of antiquity. His emphasis on the moral aspect of judgment is probably strongest in his early period because he attempts in his readings and judgments to elucidate means which will enable him to withstand philosophically the onslaught of time and surmount his dread of pain and death.

As Montaigne progresses through "De l'exercitation" and the practical lesson it contains for him, the "Apologie," and "De l'institution des enfans," he comes to depend increasingly upon his own judgment. The wisdom which he sought among the ancients he now finds within himself. The wisdom necessary to guide man's life is a personal matter. When Montaigne returns from his travels through Switzerland, Germany, and Italy, the role of judgment is completely defined. The faculty of judgment is no longer merely concerned with exterior things; rather, Montaigne has chosen to interiorize the faculty of judgment. He effects a passage from exterior to interior psychic and moral phenomena in order to better understand and interpret the exterior manifestations of human behavior which have always engrossed his attention.

Self-study constitutes a major expansion of the role of judgment. In addition to its many other duties, judgment must now study the self, that is create the self. The faculty of judgment now "judges" Montaigne and itself. Judgment's principal function has evolved from inspection to introspection.

In "Des livres," Montaigne enunciates the highly abstract and critical role of judgment. Although he does not allow his judgment to trust itself when he finds Plato's *Axiochus* a distasteful work, he nevertheless assigns to judgment the capacity and duty to interpret and determine the truth or falsehood of all appearances: "Il pense donner juste in-

end of the lecture. Montaigne agrees, but adds that Rusticus cannot be praised for wisdom since the parcel came unexpectedly and more importantly from the Emperor; his delay might have been harmful.

[1] Frame, *Montaigne's Discovery of Man*, p. 38.

terpretation aux apparences que sa conception luy presente" (II, 10, 390). If Montaigne is willing to castigate his judgment, it is because he is aware that his conception may not be as powerful as that of some of his predecessors. Judgment must frequently penetrate below the surface in order to capture the hidden and true meaning of appearances. If Montaigne's judgment differs from that of certain ancients, he willingly withholds his opinion:

> il n'est pas si sot de s'opposer à l'authorité de tant d'autres fameux jugemens anciens, qu'il tient ses regens et ses maistres, et avec lesquels il est plustost content de faillir. Il s'en prend à soy, et se condamne, ou de s'arrester à l'escorce, ne pouvant penetrer jusques au fons, ou de regarder la chose par quelque faux lustre (II, 10, 389).

However, once Montaigne turns his judgment inward, he need no longer relinquish the authority of his judgment, for it can be answerable only to itself. Although the interpretation of the fleeting appearances of the self is a more difficult task than the classification of manifestations which are external to the self, the faculty of judgment is strengthened to the extent that it can now rely not only on the presentations of its conception but also on its awareness and knowledge of internal sensations. In other words, the faculty of judgment discerns both intellectually and organically or personally; its object, although psychic and frequently ephemeral, is more concrete, more palpable, than the realm of abstract and relative knowledge with which it has had to deal. The business of self-criticism demands the participation of one's entire being.

One of the major contributing factors in the evolving role of judgment is Montaigne's belief that he judges better than most men. A strong independent strain vis-à-vis the rest of humanity and the knowledge that his judgment is an incorruptible instrument lead him to believe that he can fathom and portray himself accurately and honestly, without embellishment nor impairment. In most matters, he prefers to rely on his own judgment:

> Je n'ay guere à me prendre de mes fautes ou infortunes à autre qu'à moy. Car, en effect, je me sers rarement des advis d'autruy, si ce n'est par honneur de ceremonie, sauf où j'ay besoing d'instruction de science ou de la connoissance du faict. Mais, és choses où je n'ay à employer que le jugement, les raisons estrangeres peuvent servir à m'appuyer, mais peu à me destourner (III, 2, 792).

Montaigne's personal judgment is juxtaposed with that of others and with the principles of authority; it deals effectively with those areas of thought in which a personal opinion is not immediately verifiable. In all things except matters of fact, Montaigne's judgment, that is his ability to think well, to see clearly, and to evaluate exactly, holds him in good stead.

Much of "De la vanité" is concerned with the theme of travel. Montaigne remarks that he follows no particular plan in the course of his sightseeing. If he happens to overlook something, he willingly retraces his steps. If he does not find what he expected to see, long habit enables him to remain poised and unruffled. The measure of his sight does not often bear out the evaluations of others: "(Comme il advient souvent que les jugemens d'autruy ne s'accordent pas aux miens, et les ay trouvez plus souvant faux), je ne plains pas ma peine; j'ay apris que ce qu'on disoit n'y est point" (III, 9, 963). In the *Journal de voyage*, the secretary writes that Montaigne always distrusted the opinions of others on the convenience of foreign countries and normally discounted the advice and warnings of other travellers.[1] The examination of reason's inabilities in the "Apologie" and Montaigne's personal experience reinforce his desire to judge and see everything for himself. Self-reliance is at the heart of self-knowledge.

Montaigne contracts the scope of judgment's objects until the study of self becomes its sole preoccupation: "Et puis, me trovant entierement despourveu et vuide de toute autre matiere, je me suis presenté moymesme à moy, pour argument et pour subject" (II, 8, 364). The search for unity of being and truth is grounded in the study of self. The only thing which man can *tâter* at will, an expression which Montaigne uses frequently with reference to the self,[2] and of which he can have an immediate experience is himself. Paradoxically, the flexibility and significance of judgment is increased through its limitation to one subject.

SELF-IDENTIFICATION

The notion of judging seems to have evolved in three successive stages, on the one hand, and to have incorporated all three in varying degrees at all times, on the other. Initially, to judge is to determine critically the truth or falsehood, and the worth, of ideas and actions. To this is added the determination of good or evil inasmuch as judgment concerns itself with the moral improvement of man. Finally, to judge, a form of personal constructive criticism, is to establish for oneself a

[1] *Journal de voyage*, p. 1170.

[2] III, 3, 797: "Le mediter est un puissant estude et plein, à qui sçait se taster et employer vigoureusement: j'aime mieux forger mon ame que la meubler."

psychological and moral identity. The operation of judgment in general has already been noted.[1] The purpose of this section is to study the operation of judgment in its analysis and construction of personality and to examine some of the things Montaigne reveals about himself in relation to judgment. Montaigne judges and reflects the collective body of men and in turn he is judged by them and reflected in them.

In the study of self, the function of the faculty of judgment is to record (*enrôler*) the result of its probes of the psyche. *Enrôler* implies the existence of a *rôle* or the formation of a *rôle* upon which new information can be inscribed. Moreover, the result is dependent upon an active and incessant engagement of judgment. The faculty of judgment can no longer disengage itself at will, for it is both the object and the instrument of scrutiny. In a review article on Hugo Friedrich's *Montaigne* (Bern, 1949), M. De Man speaks of Montaigne's inability to completely transcend himself in his quest for self. Although Montaigne transcends himself in order to study himself, thereby creating a duality of being, Montaigne-observed constantly obstructs the view of Montaigne the observer: "Le premier demeure objet pour la réflexion du second; il impose sa loi à cette réflexion, jusque dans ses moindres détails; il lui enlève toute force de constance et de vérité absolue, mais non pas son caractère réfléchissant." [2]

As has been noted,[3] the solid and heavy psychological, physical, and emotional mass which constitutes man impedes the reflective analysis of judgment. Yet whatever the outcome, the "moi" of being must be discovered by the "je" ("nous sommes, je ne sçay comment, doubles en nous mesmes," II, 16, 603) before it can be studied and formulated. Self-discovery precedes self-study. Self-study leads to "connaissance de soi"; however, *savoir*, in the sense of possession, of experience of self, antedates the notion of *connaître*, and hence of *juger*. But, *juger*, in terms of self-knowledge, precedes *connaître*. Hence, *juger* and *savoir* are more closely connected than one might first expect.

There is a very important physical dimension to the reflective character of self-discovery. In discussing his study of self, Montaigne customarily speaks in physical terms. The concrete notion to which he most frequently returns is that of touch. Montaigne reaches out or rather within and literally touches his being, fashioning it, as a sculptor

[1] Chapter I, pp. 31–41.

[2] Paul De Man, "Montaigne et la transcendence," *Critique*, IX (1953), 1017.

[3] Chapter II, "The Emotional Nature of Man," pp. 54–61 and "Deficiency: A Practical Guide," pp. 62–67.

molds clay. Montaigne accepts the material aspect of being, for he senses that he grasps his "moi" sensorially.

It is interesting to note that the etymology of *savoir* is Classical Latin *sapĕre,* that is "avoir de la saveur." [1] One experiences and knows (*savoir*) oneself by judging oneself, that is by taking oneself in, by breathing oneself in, for one's inner being releases savors that are felt, smelled, and even tasted.

The faculty of judgment explores and essays (*se tâter*) the "moi." The idea of *goûter* frequently associated with the verb *tâter* in Old French is usually maintained by Montaigne.[2] Indeed, Montaigne is often highly explicit in his contention that he savors and tastes slowly, with attention and pleasure, every facet of his being as it unfolds gratuitously before his judgment or emerges because of its active inquisition:

> Le monde regarde tousjours vis à vis; moy, je replie ma veuë au dedans, je la plante, je l'amuse là. Chacun regarde devant soy; moy, je regarde dedans moy: je n'ay affaire qu'à moy, je me considere sans cesse, je me contrerolle, je me gouste. Les autres vont tousjours ailleurs, s'ils y pensent bien; ils vont tousjours avant ... moy je me roulle en moy mesme (II, 17, 641).

Montaigne's reflections in "De l'exercitation" upon his mounting awareness of himself, as he slowly recovers from unconsciousness after his fall from a horse, constitute an outstanding example of self-discovery. In a very detached manner, Montaigne thrills to the vibration of his existence; he feels himself physically and figuratively, and his reactions are his indices. His solitary conscious examination of himself, of his mind and of his body in their relationship with one another, demonstrates the physical exposure of his consciousness or "conscience de soi." Lalande describes it as an "intuition (plus ou moins complète, plus ou moins claire) qu'a l'esprit de ses états et de ses actes." [3] Littré defines it as the "sentiment de soi-même ou mode de la sensibilité générale qui nous permet de juger de notre existence: c'est ce que les métaphysiciens nomment la conscience du moi." [4]

Montaigne used to concern himself with literary and psychological facts which he found outside of himself. As he studied and analyzed these facts, he attached to them or rather detached from them some of his personality; exterior manifestations elicited his thought. As an

1 Bloch and von Wartburg, p. 568.

2 *Ibid.*, p. 618: Thibaudet and Rat, ed. *Œuvres complètes de Montaigne*, p. 1768.

3 André Lalande, *Vocabulaire technique et critique de la philosophie* (Paris, 1960), p. 173.

4 Emile Littré, *Dictionnaire de la langue française* (Paris, 1882), I, 744–745.

example, his psychological and intellectual personality may be said to have been fashioned by his reading of Plutarch's works. Michel de Montaigne was the man who expressed himself through his study and appreciation of Plutarch. In other words, Montaigne's inner being expressed itself vicariously through and among Montaigne's readings and judgments.

Now Montaigne finds that his one subject of study need be only himself. His inner being, a composite of physical, psychological, and moral determinations, can be perceived, studied, and defined. Montaigne has a physical and moral personality unlike that of any other man; his body and his spiritual interaction with it have molded his identity. Montaigne possesses himself or rather can possess himself, and his awareness of this structure of his being leads him to describe more and more personal things about himself. Montaigne becomes fully cognizant of the regressive motion which the notion of education and intellectual and psychological creation expresses etymologically: *ex*, out of, and *ducere*, to lead, draw, bring.

Montaigne's fear of the stone ("la gravelle") and general concern for his body and its state of health bring him into contact with himself. When Montaigne concludes after several experiments that three cups of mineral water will afford him eight hours of relief, his physical and psychological personality records this analysis. His being is further defined in terms of what governs it and what affords it happiness. Montaigne first discovers himself in his physical being. Daily and constant contact and interaction between the body and the psyche lead to a consciousness of self: "A force d'apprendre ce qu'il devait fuir, et ce qu'il devait rechercher, il devint conscient de lui-même." [1]

The "instrument judicatoire" which Montaigne once thought could not be found (II, 12, 585) is the faculty of judgment. Berated as unstable and uncertain in the "Apologie," judgment is now considered the one instrument capable of capturing and verifying that most intricate and elusive of subjects, man's individual personality. Montaigne's concern for the fluidity of existence, expressed throughout the *Essais* and particularly in the "Apologie," is redefined as a necessary and useful corollary to the study and knowledge of self. Initially, Montaigne saw the transitoriness of time and things as an insurmountable obstruction in the path of self-knowledge. Presently inexistent within his molecularly mutated existence and incapable of attaining

[1] Imbrie Buffum, *L'Influence du voyage de Montaigne sur les Essais* (Princeton, 1946), p. 53.

a fixed and constant being, man was condemned to a state of perpetual non-being:

> il n'y a aucune constante existence, ny de nostre estre, ny de celuy des objects. Et nous, et nostre jugement, et toutes choses mortelles, vont coulant et roulant sans cesse. Ainsin il ne se peut establir rien de certain de l'un à l'autre, et le jugeant et le jugé estans en continuelle mutation et branle (II, 12, 586).

Montaigne now perceives that motion and change, at least in so far as self-knowledge is concerned, are not only useful and necessary but also good. Change, particularly moral change, is both a part and a pattern of life. Man must constantly strive to be better, for he can improve; however, he must first know himself. In order to improve the performance of a piece of machinery, one must first familiarize oneself with all the component parts, the tolerance of each, the necessary and gradated relationship of one to the other, and the influence which they exert upon each other.

Because being is fluid, knowledge of being must also be fluid and flexible. It is in the nature of the faculty of judgment to be mobile, pliable, and perspicacious. It is admirably suited to the needs of self-knowledge because judgment comes into being through its constant contact with experience. Experience, in the sense of "connaissance" rather than that of "épreuve," constitutes a record of change. Self and judgment are inextricably bound by their organic and reciprocal interdependency.

The faculty of judgment is called upon to study man in his entirety, that is in his personal, social, and professional behavior, in his changing moods, and in the expression of his thoughts. The faculty of judgment "judges" the inner being on the basis of outward appearances. Judgment must ponder the significance of innumerable behavioral indices and determine the extent to which they are true and accurate reflections of the inner being. For Montaigne, each and every action in a man's life is motivated, and the true picture of the man is to be found not in his actions, but in what can be culled from them. Montaigne seeks the cause which activates man's behavior. Montaigne attempts to penetrate the genes of personality, of self, in order that he may be better able to predict future behavior, at least in so far as he is personally concerned.

Whether Montaigne judges himself, that is seeks his true psychological identity, in an effort to increase his control, both psychological and moral, over himself, or whether he hopes primarily to increase his capacity to deal accurately with the appearances which the world about him generates incessantly, he usually conceives of the act of judging the self in one of two opposing methods.

The first confrontation of judgment and self is a passive one; in fact, it is occasionally in spite of itself that judgment's knowledge of the self is increased:

Je ne me tiens pas bien en ma possession et disposition. Le hazard y a plus de droict que moy. L'occasion, la compaignie, le branle mesme de ma voix tire plus de mon esprit que je n'y trouve lors que je le sonde et employe à part moy.... Ceci m'advient aussi: que je ne me trouve pas où je me cherche; et me trouve plus par rencontre que par l'inquisition de mon jugement (I, 10, 41–42).

In these occurrences, there is no active inquisition on the part of judgment. The connections necessary to an understanding of a particular aspect of self are made without its knowledge or consent. Judgment faces a *fait accompli* of inquiry; it need only direct the extent and penetration of its recording; it remains free to utilize its acquisition in the future, if it deems it necessary. Montaigne's awareness and knowledge of himself is frequently acquired in this fashion.

However, because this method of research is erratic, unpredictable, and often unreliable, Montaigne finds it necessary to rely increasingly upon a constant and active research on the part of judgment. Although Montaigne's knowledge of himself is generally gained by means of intuition rather than self-analysis *per se,* that is a conscious and predetermined series of investigations of the "moi" by the "je," it must be noted that Montaigne maintains about himself an aura of constant and active self-analysis. Life may be a long, arduous, and never-ending quest for self-knowledge. Nevertheless, Montaigne is interested in the *hic et nunc* of existence. Personal happiness is the prize of triumphant self-knowledge, and happiness can only be measured in human terms, in the terms of the here and now.

Judgment is a creative faculty; Montaigne does not judge his being in dejection but in action. Judgment looks forward, not backward; it is the hope and salvation of man, not his tarnished and ineffectual past. If man is to profit from self-knowledge, judgment must actively attempt to uncover and decipher his inner being. Montaigne is incapable of methodology and rigid organization, but not of sense of purpose and *ordre.*

Man lives his life on an hourly basis, and his inner being is constantly escaping him. Man's fluid self must be "judged" instantaneously within its fluidity. Judgment may be an imperfect instrument and the object of its scrutiny an imperfection since it never *is* and maintains itself at best in a constant process of becoming. Yet, dejection breeds only futility. Hence, imperfect knowledge of oneself is still knowledge, and that is still more than most men possess. Montaigne opts for the active and self-negating role of judgment, self-negating in the sense that it limits any knowledge that it might have of other things and of itself by linking its destiny to that of man's self. The faculty of judgment will be relatively efficacious or inept, good or bad, in proportion to the amount of self-knowledge which it unearths. Judgment stands or falls in the arena of self-knowledge.

Montaigne frequently remarks upon the amount of time he, that is his judgment, spends with himself. These two distinct, yet inseparable parts of his personality, his "je" and his "moi," are constantly acting upon each other. Judgment examines, that is it judges, the "moi" in action, in motion often imperceptible to the naked eye. Only judgment can have true knowledge of the very personal and intimate "moi." Moreover, this psychological familiarity is not gained haphazardly: "Cette longue attention que j'employe à me considerer me dresse à juger aussi passablement des autres, et est peu de choses dequoy je parle plus heureusement et excusablement" (III, 13, 1053). As P. Mansell Jones remarks,[1] Montaigne is particularly anxious to point out the social implication of his undertaking. Self-knowledge increases his ability to understand, to judge others. He finds that he can often pinpoint a friend's character more easily and accurately than he might himself.

For Montaigne, the verb *dresser* and its notion of self-training and self-help is a significant one in the concept of judgment. It implies that self-knowledge is not acquired through some magic interaction of self and judgment. On the contrary, self-knowledge is the product of three mutually exclusive elements toiling in unison; they are the self, judgment, and man in general. Knowledge of the self obtained by means of judgment alone is not sufficient. Knowledge of man acquired without the participation of the self is deficient. All knowledge of the self is dependent upon its reflection in the mirror of humanity. The self does not exist in isolation; self-knowledge must be measured against knowledge of man. Hence, Montaigne attempts to train and dispose himself (*se dresser*) for a constant analysis of himself and of men about him in order to better understand the whole of humanity and to know how to improve himself intellectually, psychologically, and morally.

[1] Jones, p. 41.

Man can never know himself completely. A lifetime is not sufficient, and few men can claim the tenacity of purpose found in Montaigne: "Pour m'estre, dès mon enfance, dressé à mirer ma vie dans celle d'autruy, j'ay acquis une complexion studieuse en cela" (III, 13, 1053).

To judge always implies the creation of parallels: "mirer ma vie dans celle d'autruy." When Montaigne observes, judges another being's behavior, he immediately contrasts it with what his own might be in a similar situation. The parallel serves two purposes. On the one hand, Montaigne is apt to clarify some aspect of his personality or "inclinations internes" which lay dormant until aroused and thus discovered by personal reflection. On the other hand, once his self-knowledge is increased, his judgment can determine the degree of good or evil to be attached to the action. On the basis of these findings, it next determines whether the action shall be incorporated as a part of the self or whether attempts will be made to eradicate it: "J'estudie tout: ce qu'il me faut fuyr, ce qu'il me faut suyvre" (III, 13, 1053).

The purpose of judgment is to bring everything back to the self, to measure everything in terms of the self. Montaigne knows that he possesses an individual and "true" personality; it need only be judged, that is adjudged to be, considered, and studied. The act of judgment is one of laborious study and hence of education. To judge means not only "voir et distinguer," as important as these exercises may be individually, but also to study, and particularly in the sense of to observe meticulously, to fix one's gaze on the self attentively and thoughtfully and analyze it carefully. The acquisition of knowledge usually associated with the notion of study need not be stressed, for the body of knowledge which judgment seeks to unearth and acquire is an understanding of self and of itself. To study the self, that is to judge it, implies both the method and the goal.

Hence, to judge the self differs in degree of complexity and difficulty from the capacity to discern and distinguish within it. The self is constantly undergoing change; yet Montaigne or rather his judgment is automatically and mechanically capable of seeing and discerning the tiny particles that constitute the self as they pass before the mind's eye. Montaigne possesses the uncanny ability to ferret out opposites and degrees of difference. His judgment can separate the individual from the whole but not fix it in time in order to be able to judge it at leisure.

To judge, to study the self, requires recurrence, retention, and repetition. Judgment must remain fixed upon its object, codify disparate and recalcitrant elements, and analyze recurring change as it takes place. As soon as a new facet or fact of one's psychological and moral identity is discovered, it must be compared to the self-knowledge already in existence and its proper relationship and degree of importance ascertained. One's being escapes disintegration within the timeless and spaceless analysis of judgment.

Montaigne often reiterates the avowed purpose of his *Essais*, that is the study of man, and nowhere does he express it as forcefully or more incisively than in "De la praesumption." [1] The principal object of judgment's study is man, and it supersedes all its other activities. Montaigne decries the "know-it-all" who sits astride the epicycle of Mercury and purports to speak knowledgeably on all subjects; he knows nothing of his own:

> ces gens là n'ont peu se resoudre de la connoissance d'eux mesmes et de leur propre condition, qui est continuellement presente à leurs yeux, qui est dans eux.... ils ne sçavent comment branle ce qu'eux mesmes font branler, ny comment nous peindre et deschiffrer les ressorts qu'ils tiennent et manient eux mesmes (II, 17, 617–18).

Man must know himself, create himself, *se résoudre* on the plane of being. To judge oneself is not only a matter of *s'essayer* but also one of *se résoudre*; through repetitive trials or "essais," one becomes resolved. The goal of judgment is to resolve the dilemma of identity. One finds one's identity within oneself, not at the hands of friends nor in the world at large. One must decide, come to an agreement as to one's personality, and this is what Montaigne has in mind whenever he says "I judge myself." Everything one needs to know is within oneself, within one's life: "Escoutons y seulement; nous nous disons tout ce de quoy nous avons principalement besoing" (III, 13, 1051).

THE ROLE OF APPRAISAL

Man is a mass of motion (*branler*), and the difficulties involved in capturing the "moi" within its change have already been noted. Nevertheless, judgment controls or is capable of controlling the kinetic aspect of man's being by painting or describing and deciphering the springs which remain at its disposal.[2] For Montaigne, the interaction of

[1] II, 17, 617–618.

[2] *Peindre* et *déchiffrer* is another important example of Montaigne's frequent and abrupt constriction from the general to the particular although the action contained in *déchiffrer* is an inherent part of the more general *peindre*. Normally, one would show a gradation from *to decipher* to *to depict*, for the latter is but the representation of the results obtained by the former. This aspect of Montaigne's thinking habits has already been noted with reference to the verb *juger*. See Chapter I, "Operation of Judgment," p. 33.

judgment and self in the course of introspection needs to be recorded so that the self may attain a relative degree of permanence. It is interesting to note that in the sixteenth century and occasionally in the *Essais*,[1] the verb *peindre* also implies to write. Montaigne chooses to write about himself, to paint himself, in the *Essais*, in order to encase himself in a solid and palpable state. Early in the course of his philosophical musings, Montaigne saw the utility of writing in order to think; he also came to see the possibility and inescapability of *se penser, se créer*, inherent in the written knowledge of self:

> Moulant sur moy cette figure, il m'a fallu si souvent dresser et composer pour m'extraire, que le patron s'en est fermy et aucunement formé soy-mesmes. Me peignant pour autruy, je me suis peint en moy de couleurs plus nettes que n'estoyent les miennes premieres (II, 18, 647–648).

Montaigne and man find out who they are psychologically and morally in their attempts at self-judgment. They extract their essence through their judgment.

Similarly, Montaigne, maliciously at times one surmises, attempts to ferret out his "essential" opponent by asking him to confront himself publicly: "Au reste, quand je veux juger de quelqu'un, je luy demande combien il se contente de soy, jusques où son parler et sa besongne luy plaist" (III, 8, 918). For Montaigne, the judging of the self is officially and definitely a form of appraisal. The purpose of judging oneself, of thus obtaining that rarest of all gifts, "communication à l'estre," [2] is the concomitant evaluation of what one finds, as one would estimate the worth of an estate. It does not suffice to know oneself; one must also set an accurate and just value to one's knowledge of oneself; man must appraise himself. There is a definite difference between the realization that one reacts favorably to solicitude and unfavorably to pressure, and the appraisal of the action which it elicits. The ability to appraise, to judge the worth, the good or evil of the action, of the particular "branle," for the self, determines the viability of the reaction. Hence, the self is constructed or reconstructed little by little, judgment by judgment.

To judge the self often requires stealth. Indeed, the function of judgment is one of attentive and secretive observation. The soul and the imagination tend to obfuscate the direct penetration of judgment.

[1] Thibaudet and Rat, ed. *Œuvres complètes de Montaigne*, p. 1759. Huguet, V, 700. I, 40, 247: "J'escris mes lettres tousjours en poste, et si precipiteusement, que, quoy que je peigne insupportablement mal, j'ayme mieux escrire de ma main que d'y en employer un'autre, car je n'en trouve poinct qui me puisse suyvre, et ne les transcris jamais."

[2] Cf. Poulet, p. 15.

The faculty of judgment must lie in wait and seek to explore and discover the darker recesses of the mind. Montaigne frequently refers to the verb *épier*, and undoubtedly it is an interesting aspect of judgment's performance:

> Si chacun espioit de près les effects et circonstances des passions qui le regentent, comme j'ay faict de celle à qui j'estois tombé en partage, il les verroit venir, et ralantiroit un peu leur impetuosité et leur course (III, 13, 1051–1052).

The faculty of judgment must conceal itself and watch the self closely. Its methods are often devious according to the subject. Secretiveness and concealment are aspects of judgment in the discovery of the self because Montaigne recognizes that the soul, the self, is not an open book and that its structure is one which is based both on depth and on circumference. In other words, Montaigne visualizes the self as a construction whose structural circles or layers expand into infinity as penetration increases.

In the discovery of the self, Montaigne conceives of judgment as an instrument which probes cautiously and systematically. The faculty of judgment is neither a blunt nor a sharp instrument, and its probe of the psyche is rather like that of a seismograph. Like a seismograph, judgment records the moment of passage of every wave and the time and effect of its oscillation from one psychic layer to another. Judgment never comes into direct contact with the whole of the self. In receives only waves and reverberations of the true being. It is for this reason that judgment must be a highly accurate recorder of the inner self: "il faut un jugement vif et bien trié pour l'appercevoir" (III, 2, 787).

Floyd Gray has astutely remarked that Montaigne "imagine dans le corps et dans l'âme des zones qui marquent le passage entre l'extérieur et l'intérieur, qui indiquent la profondeur qu'atteint une sensation venant du dehors." [1] Montaigne invariably sees man in action, for it is action which gives him being, and each and every action is a test of the inner being. Its effect is felt throughout the self, and the role of judgment is to record the impact and the reflection within the "replis internes" of the self.

In order to communicate with the "replis internes" or successive layers which compose man's personality, the faculty of judgment must verify and test them, *toucher au-dedans*, and more importantly, explore and ascertain their depth and composition, *sonder*. Judgment is a sounding-rod, an instrument capable of activating the self in its totality

[1] Floyd Gray, *Le Style de Montaigne* (Paris, 1958), p. 159.

and of measuring its true reality in its very displacement:

> ceux qui nous jugent et touchent au dedans, ne font pas grand recette de la lueur de noz actions publiques et voyent que ce ne sont que filets et pointes d'eau fine rejaillies d'un fond au demeurant limonneux et poisant (III, 2, 787).

The exposure of what one is or of what one might be depends upon the activation of a heavy and muddy core. To sound, to judge, this inner and dormant mass is to give it life, bring it into being by disengaging it from its nothingness. Judgment prods and disturbs the self, for revelation lies within movement.

The movement of the self proceeds in two directions. At times, as in the preceding lines, judgment is able to test the self as it unravels itself and trickles to the surface. This movement is an outward one, progressing from the inner core to the outer layer in a series of increasing and expanding concentric circles. In general, Montaigne contends that one man's knowledge of another is limited to what can be perceived within the last superficial circle. However, the directional pattern which Montaigne prefers, recommends, and adopts is the one which operates in reverse order. He imagines man's personality to be a pool, the depth and color of which are initially unknown. When he approaches a stranger, his judgment formulates the proper question which will act as a stone dropped into a pool of water. As the stone descends, rings emerge; nevertheless, the stone continues its path, and Montaigne's eyes or judgment remain fixed upon it. In other words, Montaigne espies the self in its absence as it recedes from view. He is aware that the silences of an author, for example, are frequently more significant than what he actually writes.

The notion of *sonder*, literally and figuratively, is constantly associated in Montaigne's mind with the concept of judgment, especially as a means of obtaining self-knowledge. For Montaigne, *sonder* is perhaps the verb and descriptive action which best typifies the activities of judgment. For every action, there must be a sounding, a judgment in order to determine its significance, place, and value within the context of man's personality. In "De la gloire," Montaigne appropriately defines "le jugement de nos inclinations et de nos actions" as "la plus difficile matiere et la plus importante qui soit" (II, 16, 607).

In order to arrive at a true and composite understanding of a man's internal identity, each psychological and moral manifestation of being must be judged individually. Initially, Montaigne felt that it was not feasible to portray, that is to solidify, a man's identity on the basis of separate judgments. Only a few men can be properly judged on the basis of one or two appearances. Montaigne considers Cato the Younger to be an excellent example:

qui en a touché une marche, a tout touché; c'est une harmonie de sons très-accordans, qui ne se peut démentir. A nous, au rebours, autant d'actions, autant faut-il de jugemens particuliers. Le plus seur, à mon opinion, seroit de les rapporter aux circonstances voisines, sans entrer en plus longue recherche et sans en conclurre autre consequence (II, 1, 317).

By contrast, it is interesting to note how confident Montaigne has become of being able to know man on the basis of judgment. In the essay "De l'inconstance de nos actions," written in 1572–1574, he does not feel that man can be reorganized into an intelligible and improvable whole. He despairs of man's judicious capability, for he senses in man an inability or unwillingness to penetrate exterior appearances. Far too many important aspects of personality escape the reach of "une veuë grossière comme est la nostre" (III, 12, 1013). Only the "filets et pointes d'eau fine" previously mentioned reach judgment's retina.

As Montaigne's confidence in his judgment and in the training and improvability of that of man in general heightens, his use of visual imagery with regard to self-knowledge increases proportionately. Judgment is frequently cloaked in the garb of sight. Expressions with *oeil, yeux, regard, vue, voir,* and *regarder,* consistently represent the graphic relationship of judgment to the self. In "De l'experience," Montaigne remarks that he was ideally suited by judgment and inclination to be a king's counselor. Indeed, for Montaigne, a king's counselor must not only give advice in public matters, but also realize that the examination of his personal and private conduct is a service of far greater value. Montaigne would interrogate the king's self and judge his conduct, "observant pas à pas, à toute oportunité, et en jugeant à l'oeil piece à piece, simplement et naturellement, luy faisant voyr quel il est.... J'eusse eu assez de fidelité, de jugement et de liberté pour cela" (III, 13, 1055). Verbs of examination, for example *épier, estimer,* and *contreroller,* reinforce at every turn the notion that the observation, discovery, and guidance of the self are entrusted to the faculty of judgment.

Montaigne's usage of exterior and interior imagery in order to describe the composition of man finds its corollary in the physical, visual structure and description of judgment. To judge oneself is to keep one's eyes trained on oneself, observing and examining everything that flashes before them. Man's judgment, his critical faculty, must penetrate the outer core of being, man as he presents himself to the world, and analyze and evaluate each encrustation which it penetrates and removes: "Pourquoy, estimant un homme, l'estimez vous tout enveloppé et empaqueté? ... Il le faut juger par luy mesme, non par ses atours" (I, 42, 251).

The notion of knowledge of human nature, if not self-knowledge, is present in all of Montaigne's writing, from the earliest to the last essays. One tends to forget this when confronted by Montaigne's dramatic realization that judgment is not only capable of providing self-knowledge, but that this is also its primary purpose inasmuch as its own viability depends upon change, growth, and improvement. Montaigne has always sought to judge, that is to know, understand, and evaluate human behavior, and human nature. He seeks to know and understand human nature even when emulation is beyond his ability or his inclination:

Moy, je considere aucuns hommes fort loing au-dessus de moy, noméement entre les anciens; et encores que je reconnoisse clairement mon impuissance à les suyvre de mes pas, je ne laisse pas de les suyvre à veue et juger les ressorts qui les haussent ainsin (II, 32, 730).

Montaigne has always considered judgment to be the faculty with which to "juger les ressorts" of human nature. To judge man intellectually, psychologically, and morally continues to imply a certain amount of control which one exercises upon oneself and others.

One judges oneself not only to know who one is but also to fashion oneself according to a pattern evolved both by judgment and conscience. For Montaigne, the constructive criticism and judgment of human activity always remain at the forefront of his thought. It is a slow and cautious enterprise, requiring a great deal of critical acumen, of judgment: "quand on juge d'une action particuliere, il faut considerer plusieurs circonstances et l'homme tout entier qui l'a produicte, avant la baptizer" (II, 11, 406). When Montaigne emerged confident and revitalized from the "Apologie," the only change which he brought to his search for knowledge of human nature, of being, was his decision to "judge" it within himself.

Montaigne consistently judges man in moral terms. All actions and all parts of man are distinguishable on the basis of good and evil. The faculty of judgment forces and enables man to participate in a perpetual "examen de conscience." Underlying the concept of judgment throughout the *Essais* is the persistent but undeclared notion that man constantly faces a tribunal, that is judgment, a body which must pass judgment on the reality, morality, and feasibility of self. By temperament and training, Montaigne is an advocate and a judge:

Un jugement roide et hautain et qui juge sainement et seurement, il use à toutes mains des propres exemples ainsi que de chose estrangere, et tesmoigne franchement de luy comme de chose tierce (III, 8, 921).

His knowledge of legal vocabulary permeates his descriptions and discussions of judgment. The terms *tesmoigner*, *tesmoing*, and *comparaître* are frequently used to denote the close observation, the witnessing of the self, carried out by the faculty of judgment.[1] In "De la praesumption," he remarks that, to his knowledge, the sentiment of glory, of inordinate pride, is not a part of his personality. Moreover, if glory superficially moves him on occasion, it is due to the treachery of his nature, for, of its own, glory has no body "qui comparoisse à la veuë de mon jugement" (II, 17, 618). In a sense, the faculty of judgment is constantly holding court; it calls upon man's various actions to explain themselves and analyse themselves with the help of judgment. Man is constantly in litigation with himself in order to know himself.

It might also be said that man is consistently at odds with himself, never desiring the same thing twice, never becoming fully aware of where his happiness lies. Interminably inconsistent, he is always reaching out for the desired goal, while full of trepidation, indifference, and frequently remorse. Jeanson maintains, for example, that Montaigne seems to have been unable to resolve the dilemma of privacy of self which his object of self-portraiture posed for him.[2] He finds that Montaigne fears the gaze of an unknown public which will have easy access to his naked soul. It seems that Jeanson's thesis is, at best, mildly adventurous. Certainly, Montaigne feels the impact of his portrait upon his self-formation:

Je sens ce proffit inesperé de la publication de mes meurs qu'elle me sert aucunement de regle. Il me vient par fois quelque consideration de ne trahir l'histoire de ma vie. Cette publique declaration m'oblige de me tenir en ma route, et à ne desmentir l'image de mes conditions (III, 9, 958).

He may feel somewhat constrained and notice the loss of a certain amount of psychological and moral mobility. However, one of Montaigne's greatest intellectual gifts is that of communication, which also happens to be his lifelong endeavor, the essential aspect of his book, the purpose of his rumination and self-cogitation. Montaigne, self-judged, stands self-communicated, self-created.

[1] II, 16, 609: "tous ces jugemens qui se font des apparences externes sont merveilleusement incertains et douteux; et n'est aucun si asseuré tesmoing comme chacun à soy-mesme."

[2] Jeanson, pp. 29 and 58.

In "Du dementir" [1] and again in the "Au lecteur" [2] of 1580, Montaigne states that his book, that is his likeness, his portrait, is for the corner of a library, accessible to friends and relatives who may wish to know him or reacquaint themselves with him. However, in "De l'art de conferer," written in 1585–1588, he declares: "Je prens si grand plaisir d'estre jugé et cogneu, qu'il m'est comme indifferent en quelle des deux formes je le soys" (III, 8, 902). Earlier, in "De la praesumption," he remarks: "Par ces traits de ma confession, on en peut imaginer d'autres à mes despens. Mais, quel que je me face connoistre, pourveu que je me face connoistre tel que je suis, je fay mon effect" (II, 17, 636). There is no doubt that Montaigne approves the dispersion and availability of his portrait. Montaigne does not fear the knowledge which others may gain of his inner being; he fears erroneous interpretation. Indeed, in "De la vanité," he declares that he would willingly come back from the dead in order to give the lie to those who might misjudge him, even if it were in his favor.[3]

Montaigne goes to great lengths in order to be exact, to paint his self-portrait as accurately as possible. One must not forget that the reader is not the only observer of Montaigne's self. Montaigne is also a spectator of himself, and his written and solidified projection of himself is a measure of his judgment and of its ability to know him truthfully. Montaigne must learn from himself, from within himself. Accuracy and self-doubt are essential aspects of a self-centered, in the positive sense of the term, morality which bases itself on the premise that judgment is an organic entity which grows and improves in accordance with the tenor of the knowledge which it obtains of itself. Montaigne's primary concern is that of being, of consciousness of the self and knowledge of existence in one's eyes and in those of others. Permanence is obtained by means of judgment.

For Montaigne, knowledge of the self and of others is based upon the incessant acts of judgment. In order to know, one must judge. To judge becomes synonymous with knowledge of the self. However, knowledge of the self *per se* does not imply correction and improvement of self; for Montaigne, only *juger* conveys that meaning. He remarks that he seeks only truth and that he embraces it no matter where he finds it. In the course of social interaction, one should "judge" openly and honestly: "Toutefois il est certes malaisé d'y attirer les hommes

[1] II, 18, 647.
[2] "Au lecteur," p. 9.
[3] III, 9, 961.

de mon temps; ils n'ont pas le courage de corriger, par ce qu'ils n'ont pas le courage de souffrir à l'estre" (III, 8, 902). In a sense, judgment, that is true and accurate judgment, is a form of censure; to judge the self always implies correction and the loss of some conscious aspect of the psychological and moral self. Judgment is more than mere knowledge; it is changing, mobile knowledge. Improvement of the self is based on a certain loss of self, no matter how valid judgment may have deemed it to be. It is for this reason that creation of the self, psychologically and morally, is an inescapable and most important aspect of the role of judgment.

In "De l'inconstance de nos actions," Montaigne concedes that his soul has as many aspects as there are positions in which he places it. He does not always say the same things about himself because he does not consistently look at himself in the same light. Indeed, Montaigne finds it immensely difficult, if not altogether impossible, to grasp himself as a whole. Only aspects of himself present themselves before his judgment: "Je n'ay rien à dire de moy, entierement, simplement et solidement, sans confusion et sans meslange, ny en un mot. *Distingo* est le plus universel membre de ma logique" (II, 1, 319).

Montaigne is unable to survey the whole of his being because he visualizes it in its multiplicity. Hence, Montaigne's molecular vision is as important a phenomenon as his antithetical mode of thinking. Although opposites come together for Montaigne, their molecular structure does not escape him nor is a void or blind spot created for the discovery, or what might better be termed the recovery, of self-knowledge and hence of the self.

Montaigne's concept of judgment is the product of his innate molecular vision. For Montaigne, to judge is to distinguish, and to distinguish is to seek and immobilize the initial essence of things, the reality and truth of being. Montaigne's vision or judgment is a molecular one because every aspect of life known to man, physical, psychological, and moral, consists of infinitesimal particles which in and of themselves do not constitute wholes which can be recognized by the naked eye. However, Montaigne is innately capable of grasping, of judging the whole in its diversity, in its infinity. As Strowski notes, "il a donc, à un très haut degré, le discernement des indiscernables." [1]

Montaigne finds being at its source. He seeks *the* molecule, the truth which explains and gives meaning to all the others. Montaigne seeks

[1] Strowski, *Montaigne*, p. 155.

not permanence, but the origin of permanence. For Montaigne, discernment precedes thought; Descartes's *cogito* is first and foremost *distingo ergo sum:* I distinguish, I judge, therefore I am. Montaigne does not sense anguish in the face of change and fluidity of being, for he seeks true being in change.

In "Des boyteux," Montaigne adopts Sebond's seemingly antithetical system of producing sound judgment.[1] He tells a nobleman who complains of the vehemence of his exhortations that "vous sentant bandé et preparé d'une part, je vous propose l'autre de tout le soing que je puis, pour esclarcir vostre jugement, non pour l'obliger" (III, 11, 1011). The significant aspect of Montaigne's forcible presentation of an entirely opposite course of action lies in his belief that the nobleman's area of selectivity is increased. Truth lies within the domain of *esclarcir*, not of *obliger*. Montaigne's endeavor to distend leads to the intended and true constriction.

The faculty of judgment is the ability to see unity in its diversity. It has been imaginatively noted that Montaigne's critical apparatus acts as a solvent upon the material which it attacks; like an acid, for instance, it disengages, one by one, the smaller stones which form a greater rock.[2] Montaigne's judgment constantly disintegrates and pulverizes existence in order to find and bare the truth or falsehood, good or evil, of the socially oriented and determined psychological, intellectual, and moral inner being of man. Montaigne's awareness of the disparity which exists in all of life and his own natural capacity and drive to pursue psychical reality in its atomic structure constitute the essential bond which activates and propels the faculty of judgment to the position of eminence which it occupies in his conception of the soul.

It is because Montaigne recognizes that his greatest asset is the ability to distinguish and to discern that the faculty of judgment is visualized and conceptualized as that specific capacity. In other words, the origin of the role of judgment, for Montaigne and for man, is found in Montaigne's "capacité de trier le vray ... et cett'humeur libre de n'assubjectir aisément ma creance" (II, 17, 641). Constructive curiosi-

[1] Sebond in *Œuvres complètes de Michel de Montaigne*, ed. Arthur Armaingaud (Paris, 1924–1941, IX, 118–119: "Si on nous presente pour approuver ou nier quelque proposition qui se puisse concevoir par la raison: nous devons soudain considerer celle qui luy est directement opposee et contraire. Et parce que l'une de celles-là sera par necessité vraye, l'autre fausse: il nous faudra pour ne faillir point au chois les comparer premierement ensemble, et puis à l'homme."

[2] Alexandre Micha, "Montaigne et le drame de l'intellect," *Mercure de France*, 303 (1948), 459.

ty, doubt, and criticism of oneself and of others, that is the capacity to see distinctions, to sift and select the truth, constitute not only the definition but also the role of judgment, man's critical faculty.

THE PROBLEM OF ESSENCE AND SELF-AWARENESS

It is highly significant that Montaigne not only finds the role of judgment within himself but also chooses to pattern its functions according to the activities which it has exercised in the formulation and guidance of his inner being. There is a constancy in the remarks which Montaigne makes about his personality. Inasmuch as judgment is responsible for the creation of personal psychological identity, one finds that, for Montaigne at least, nature plots the course of judgment, that is Montaigne's judgment does not determine his identity. One of the most telling passages with regard to Montaigne's self-discovery and self-revelation is found in "Du repentir":

> Je fay coustumierement entier ce que je fay et marche tout d'une piece; je n'ay guere de mouvement qui se cache et desrobe à ma raison, et qui ne se conduise à peu près par le consentement de toutes mes parties, sans sedition intestine; mon jugement en a la coulpe ou la louange entiere; et la coulpe qu'il a une fois, il l'a tousjours, car quasi dès sa naissance il est un: mesme inclination, mesme route, mesme force. Et en matiere d'opinions universelles, dès l'enfance je me logeay au poinct où j'avois à me tenir (III, 2, 790).

These lines give credence to Gray's contention that there is an essential unity to Montaigne, an assumption that seriously impedes a chronological approach to the development of Montaigne's personality.[1] Yet, as Frame remarks, the solution to the problem is one of terminology rather than methodology.[2] The substitution of the term *revelation* for that of *development* arrests semantic discussions and recasts in its proper light the unfolding of Montaigne's personality.

More importantly, if Montaigne's nature does mold his identity, it may become increasingly necessary to speak of a certain psychological determinism in Montaigne's approach to the discovery of the self by means of judgment. On the one hand, judgment is responsible for the formulation of Montaigne's being, of his personality. The term *coulpe* or blame recalls the moral notion of the tribunal which is an organic

[1] Floyd Gray, "The Unity of Montaigne in the *Essais*," *Modern Language Quarterly*, XXII (1961), 86.

[2] Donald M. Frame, "What Next in Montaigne Studies?," *French Review*, XXXVI (1963), 581.

part of the *Essais*. On the other hand, Montaigne is as he is or rather he has become what he was, for his judgment and therefore his personality have not changed since his birth. For Montaigne, nature or inclination and judgment cannot be disassociated one from the other. In "De la praesumption," he declares that he owes his ability for sifting truth to none other than himself: "les plus fermes imaginations que j'aye, et generalles, sont celles qui, par maniere de dire, nasquirent avec moy. Elles sont naturelles et toutes miennes" (II, 17, 641). He found them within himself; the role of judgment was to solidify and exteriorize his personality by guiding it in its contacts with the world of men and ideas. Judgment and hence psychological identity is pre-determined to the extent that it is limited by nature. It is for this reason that the patterning of oneself after one's nature becomes increasingly important in Montaigne's conception of man and life. The function of judgment is the discovery of man's innate nature. As the word *coulpe* indicates, responsibility for self accrues to the faculty of judgment.

In the course of self-portraiture, Montaigne often remarks that his inclination or nature and his judgment agree on the matter at hand. In "De la ressemblance des enfans aux peres," he analyzes his reactions to internal, that is spiritual, suffering as opposed to that occasioned by bodily injury or malady. He finds that spiritual pain afflicts him much less than bodily pain, "partie par jugement .... partie par une complexion stupide et insensible que j'ay aux accidens qui ne donnent à moy de droit fil, laquelle complexion j'estime l'une des meilleures pieces de ma naturelle condition" (II, 37, 738). Indeed, Montaigne seeks to level any contention that might exist between his nature and his judgment. He presents to the world the image of a man who is in control of himself, a man who "marche tout d'une piece." By a subtle balance of nature and judgment, Montaigne's psychology remains unimpaired by inner friction. In several cases, Montaigne hastens to add that his judgment and his inclination are in agreement. For him, inner harmony is the goal of judgment and the product of self-knowledge.

Occasionally, as in "De la cruauté," Montaigne states that his judgment differs from his nature and more significantly that his nature or his conduct is better than his judgment as a means of realizing and guiding himself. Since early childhood, he has abhorred vices. Judgment confirms him in his otherwise instinctive dislike of vices. However, were it not for instinct or conscience, he might be induced into being what his judgment sagaciously and dutifully condemns:

> Je diray un monstre, mais je le diray pourtant: je trouve par là, en plusieurs choses, plus d'arrest et de reigle en mes meurs qu'en mon opinion, et ma concupiscence moins desbauchée que ma raison (II, 11, 407).

It was not until after 1588 that *opinion* replaced *jugement.* The substitution of *opinion* for *jugement* seems to mitigate the original force of the statement. Nevertheless, it is a clear indication that Montaigne is not always ruled by the knowledge of himself obtained by judgment. Montaigne's instinctive moral conduct serves to keep his intellectual judgment in check. Judgment studies human nature not only because it is its principal opponent in the formation of moral man, but also because it needs to learn of itself. Judgment and nature coalesce into one being, the one reinforcing the other; the one mark of preeminence which consistently identifies the faculty of judgment is its recognition of knowledge and abilities superior to its own, no matter what the source.

Although the faculty of judgment seeks knowledge of the self and of itself, the acquisition of self-knowledge does not always enable judgment to control the self and to correct it. Frequently, self-knowledge does not lead to psychological and moral tranquillity and happiness. At best, judgment can only note and record; it is helpless to do more, for nature proves to be the more powerful of the two:

> Rampant au limon de la terre, je ne laisse pas de remerquer, jusques dans les nuës, la hauteur inimitable d'aucunes ames héroïques. C'est beaucoup pour moy d'avoir le jugement reglé, si les effects ne le peuvent estre, et maintenir au moins cette maistresse partie exempte de corruption. C'est quelque chose d'avoir la volonté bonne, quand les jambes me faillent (I, 37, 225).

Montaigne allows a vast difference between errors of thought and errors of conduct. Man's judgment recognizes within him moral and psychological deficiencies which he is unable to combat due to an all too pervasive nature or because of a lack of willingness or fortitude. For Montaigne, the significant aspect of man's moral existence is the awareness of evil, not concomitantly nor necessarily the avoidance of it. A sound judgment must identify and categorize evil whenever and wherever it finds it: "Il n'est vice veritablement vice qui n'offence, et qu'un jugement entier n'accuse" (III, 2, 784). As Montaigne indicates in "De la cruauté," judgment can maintain itself above debauchery, even above a baser nature. In his youth, his judgment condemned his vices, "mais c'est tout; car, au demourant, j'y apporte trop peu de resistance" (II, 11, 407).

Even when unable to avoid the pitfalls of life, the self remains independent and free if judgment remains aloof and clear-eyed, recording the action, the inner turmoil, the struggle which ensues between self and conscience, and the feelings of guilt and inadequacy which remain. If judgment can accuse the self, its inability to restrain it is not a capitulation nor a condemnation of its role and powers. The desire to confront frankly what one does not have the courage to execute or undertake is a worthy and commendable quality. When man's will fails or leaves him, good will becomes his best defense. Judgment probes and guides the self so that it may be free and accordingly content. It cannot err if it abides by the rules of its formation and operation, for knowledge and freedom of self are found and firmly rooted in self-awareness.

THE NATURE OF MOVEMENT AND PERSONALITY

One of the more disarming and engaging aspects of the search for the self and expanding self-portrait are Montaigne's claims to the effect that one of his major faults is that of irresolution. In "De la vanité," he broadens this tenet to include all of humanity: "ce plaisir de voyager porte tesmoignage d'inquietude et d'irresolution. Aussi sont ce nos maistresses qualitez, et praedominantes" (III, 9, 966). Montaigne sees man in constant agitation and restlessness (*inquietude*), yet unable to resolve himself to act in one way or another (*irresolution*). In "De la praesumption," he describes this lack of resolution as a "cicatrice." Uncertainty and lack of decisiveness permeate his being: "L'incertitude de mon jugement est si également balancée en la pluspart des occurrences, que je compromettrois volontiers à la decision du sort et des dets" (II, 17, 638). Montaigne is constantly drawn between *inquietude* or the desire to act and *irresolution* or the inability to act decisively.

For Montaigne, the world is infinitely mobile; motion best characterizes its constitution. Man is in constant motion; hence, it is difficult to depict him as he is. Montaigne himself is a remarkable example of perpetual movement. Both physically and intellectually, his being is a restless entity. He finds it difficult to remain "tout d'une piece" even in ceremonials: "je ne suis jamais venu à bout que quelque piece des miennes n'extravague tousjours; encore que j'y sois assis, j'y suis peu rassis" (III, 13, 1085). Montaigne sees movement as an essential part of life. Indeed, his concept of judgment is born in motion and its formation and operation is the product of movement.

Movement is necessary for the operation of judgment as motion, for some people, is an inseparable part of thinking. There can be no discovery of self without motion. Yet, Montaigne senses and deplores the lack of *ordre* which perpetual and unguided motion implies. If one were once able to resolve oneself, to choose an identity and a firm and permanent stance in life, the self-knowledge which judgment might extricate from one's being would increase proportionately. Montaigne is aware that the displacement of that which is observed, that is the self, limits the knowledge of the self which the observer, that is judgment, attempts to obtain. In addition, the observer does not remain immobile in time and space; the modifications which it undergoes affect its analysis of the "moi." Montaigne senses that the inherent fluidity of his judgment and his being places obstacles before his self-knowledge. The portrait can never be a true reflection of the real man:

> En mes escris mesmes je ne retrouve pas tousjours l'air de ma premiere imagination; je ne sçay ce que j'ay voulu dire, et m'eschaude souvent à corriger et y mettre un nouveau sens, pour avoir perdu le premier, qui valloit mieux. Je ne fay qu'aller et venir: mon jugement ne tire pas tousjours avant; il flotte, il vague (II, 12, 549).

One never finds oneself again as one once was. To judge oneself is to chisel a block of stone; each falling chip is lost (*perdu*) to the whole.

Hence, and paradoxically, *tirer avant*, that is movement with a fixed sense of direction, is opposed to *flotter*, *vaguer*, that is fluidity, unchannelled displacement. Fluidity and fixity are constantly at odds in Montaigne's thought, although he usually favors fluidity. Only superficially does he seem to deplore his judgment's inability to go forward, for the resulting loss of self-knowledge is more than compensated for by the wanderings of judgment. Motion must know no course if it is to enhance judgment's knowledge of being. If judgment moved in a fixed direction, the erection of the "moi" would naturally be more rapid. However, the "moi" would evolve according to a predetermined pattern which might not necessarily be the true one. Moreover, only the conscious aspects of being would be ascertained. In addition, important aspects of the self would remain unknown, totally ignored, or what is worse, discarded.

Inquietude and *irresolution* maintain a precarious but essential balance which enables judgment to detect more self-knowledge than it might otherwise cull from set probes. Judgment need not, indeed must not, go forward in order to obtain true "communication à l'estre." By the same token, Montaigne habitually chooses to add to his original writings rather than correct or rewrite them: "J'adjouste, mais je ne corrige pas" (III, 9, 941). What has virtually always been correctly understood as an unfathomable labyrinthine mode of thought is essentially Montaigne's means of preserving and presenting all of himself to his reader. Corrections and erasures belie the true being.

Montaigne maintains that a man cannot be quartered and parceled. In order to know man, one must judge him in his entirety. In its association with the self, the faculty of judgment touches upon the most intimate, personal part of being. In the course of its analysis of self, it grows and improves accordingly. Judgment not only affords a passage to being, a "communication à l'estre"; it also becomes the being which can be recognized by friend and reader alike.

By judging himself and others, Montaigne forges himself a personality, an identity of recognizable likes and dislikes, virtues and faults, actions and reactions. Montaigne so associates the faculty of judgment with the development of an intellectual, psychological, and moral personality that the eventual identification of one with the other is inevitable. The "je" and the "moi" cannot be distinguished the one from the other; they fuse together and represent man's total personality, both physical and psychological. *Le jugement*, that part of man which can attract and fascinate other men, is the sum total of all of a man's distinguishing features.

Hence, judgment can be an all-inclusive term and Montaigne sometimes uses it in the way one might use the general terms *mind* or *people*. In "De la phisionomie," Montaigne remarks that he dislikes to hurt people, even when it is a question of reason and justice. He loathes criminal condemnations and does not attend them when possible. During his stay in Rome in 1581, he saw the execution of the bandit Catena and of two murderous brothers.[1] Thereafter, he refused to attend. He disapproves of severe punishment as a means to rectify wrongs:

> Les jugements ordinaires s'exasperent à la vengeance par l'horreur du meffaict. Cela mesme refroidit le mien: l'horreur du premier meurtre m'en faict craindre un second, et la haine de la premiere cruauté m'en faict hayr toute imitation (III, 12, 1041).

In other words, ordinary people and their temperaments are incited to violence and vengeance by the evil and atrocity of the deed. In this passage, Montaigne is referring to a whole and distinct person, not specifically to what has been referred to solely as the faculty of judgment, man's critical faculty. In these lines, it is interesting to note the rapid and significant progression from *jugements* to *le mien* to *me*. Montaigne pits his judgment, that is his entire person, against that of

[1] *Journal de voyage*, pp. 1210–1211.

others. The restrictive *le mien* is immediately expanded into the general and entire person, that is *me* and hence Montaigne. His use of judgment implies a complex of intellectual, psychological, and moral emotions, sensitivities, and responses. In brief, judgment here is being.

THE FUNCTION OF EXPERIENCE

Montaigne devotes an entire essay to the subject of experience. This essay, which chronologically follows "De l'institution des enfans" and the "Apologie de Raimond Sebond," constitutes one of the more important phases of Montaigne's "philosophical" development. In fact, "De l'experience" is frequently considered as representative of Montaigne's definitive philosophy. The opposition of reason and experience which creates the thematic unity of the essay also aligns the notion of experience with that of judgment. Without dealing specifically and solely with this essay, it is necessary to study the relationship of judgment and experience in order to understand more fully the concept of judgment in Montaigne.

Experience is a highly significant aspect of judgment; indeed, judgment and experience may be considered as corollary and interdependent notions in Montaigne's conceptualization of man's higher faculties. In "De l'institution des enfans," Montaigne stresses the formation of judgment, an intellectual and moral faculty, and the means to acquire this faculty. Specifically, he emphasizes the presence of the physical and psychological world which surrounds man. Judgment must be exposed to a variety of phenomena. It seeks the acquisition of practical knowledge, practical in the sense that one distinguishes theory from practice and also practical in the sense that it is useful for the beholder. Judgment is not only formed of the practical side of life; it must also be able to make psychological and moral use of what it acquires. In many respects, judgment is the faculty which represents the non-intellectual aspect of life, that part of life which cannot be fathomed or rendered abstractly and intellectually, that part of life that must be experienced rather than reasoned. For Montaigne, being and life cannot be reasoned; they are experienced.

In "De l'experience," Montaigne reasons that man has only two means at his disposal for the acquisition of knowledge, reason and experience:

Il n'est desire plus naturel que le desir de connoissance. Nous essayons tous les moyens qui nous y peuvent mener. Quand la raison nous faut, nous y employons l'experience (III, 13, 1041).

Reason represents abstract theorizing, while experience constitutes the first-hand, practical knowledge which man can have of intellectual, psychological, and moral phenomena. For Montaigne, experience implies the trial or test (*épreuve*) of something rather than knowledge acquired through long acquaintance and observation.[1] However, the latter meaning is never totally absent, for recurrence of *épreuve* results in demonstrable and verifiable "connaissance."

Like judgment, experience is actively sought; one does not submit to experience nor does one conduct experiments. On the contrary, man gives his being to experience. Experience does not imply experiment, for Montaigne is not interested in demonstrating or verifying something. The term which perhaps best describes Montaigne's notions of judgment and experience is *disponibilité*.

Montaigne senses his being by means of experience, of judgment, not by means of reason. Reason is an unchanging force. Its object or objects are immovable; as a spectator, it cannot act upon the objects which it scrutinizes; it can only theorize. Judgment or practical reason is an actor, a performer. Its objects can be altered; in other words, judgment concerns itself with everything that can be affected and changed by human action and experience. Hence, judgment is the material experience of being, and to judge is to be in perpetual, "experimental" contact with oneself. Self-knowledge is experience of self, that is "épreuve," "essai," of self.

To judge, whether it be one's being or the work of a poet, is to experience, to feel surely and unequivocally, a reaction within oneself. Because of its organic structure, judgment is the faculty which experiences change, which tests appearances and sensations which affect man's being. Experience is both "épreuve" and "connaissance," as judgment is the presently spontaneous and instantaneous as well as the composite of man's acquired behavioral knowledge. Judgment is the coupling of natural reason and intelligence with experience, in both senses of the term. Reason is an unchanging faculty. Judgment is a progressive form of reason, which undergoes change and brings about change as it experiences. As Montaigne evolves and revolves through the *Essais*, he tends more and more to place judgment under the control and aegis of experience.

It is interesting to note that as early as the composition of the "Apologie de Raimond Sebond" Montaigne tends to refute judgments

[1] W. G. Moore, "Montaigne's Notion of Experience," *The French Mind: Studies in Honor of Gustave Rudler* (Oxford, 1952), 38.

or opinions which do not have the authority of personal experience and knowledge upon which to base themselves. He remarks that his father actively sought the acquaintance of learned men and that he treated them and their pronouncements as emanating from divine wisdom, "et avec d'autant plus de reverence et de religion qu'il avoit moins de loy d'en juger, car il n'avoit aucune connoissance des lettres, non plus que ses predecesseurs" (II, 12, 415). One frequently forgets that Montaigne does not dismiss formal learning. Entirely too much has been made of Montaigne's haphazard, impressionistic, and dilettante intellectual excursions and criticism. For Montaigne, self-reliance is the touchstone of knowledge and self-knowledge. However, what one tends to overlook is the fact that it is an educated, "experienced," self-reliance.

Self-reliance is the goal of self-knowledge. It is also the means by which judgment obtains knowledge of the self. Confidence in oneself is born of self-"practice," as Montaigne might say, that is repetitious exercise, acquaintance, and experience of one's being. Based on daily and personal experience, the role of judgment is to find out and determine what one can expect of oneself physically, but more importantly and almost exclusively, intellectually, psychologically, and morally. For Montaigne, the recognition of inner fiber and self-potential is a wholly physical one. In fact, Montaigne tends to redefine man in terms of his nature, a nature whose roots he finds deeply implanted in man's body. In "De l'art de conferer," he remarks that "c'est tousjours à l'homme que nous avons affaire, duquel la condition est merveilleusement corporelle" (III, 8, 909).

Montaigne's body, especially as it manifests itself in the varying states of his health, leads him to recognize the physical contours and possibilities of his physical being and eventually those of his psychological and moral self. Phenomenologically as well as stylistically, the abstract progresses and emanates from the concrete, the one firmly rooted in the other. As Buffum indicates,[1] Montaigne's health is at the basis of his growing awareness of the need and utility of grounding one's knowledge in intimate and personal experience. During his trip through Germany, Switzerland, and Italy, Montaigne recognizes the value of keeping a detailed account of his reactions to the water which he imbibes at the various baths in which he sojourns. In fact, Montaigne's journey is the one instance in which it can be said that Montaigne literally conducts experiments. If four cups of water enable

[1] Buffum, p. 42.

him to discharge a stone within a matter of seven hours with a minimum of effort and pain, he records this result in his *Journal.* The following week, he tests the effectiveness of three cups of water from the same location. Moreover, his written account of the various doses and the relief which they produce enable him to compare one bath to another, one experience to another.

By means of physical experiments and experiences, Montaigne learns to regulate his being. His judgment acquires immediate and trustworthy knowledge of what makes him feel well and what leaves him weak, unrelieved, and in pain. No one can judge better than he the extent of the effects which he experiences, for it is his entire being which participates in and responds to the individual test or experience. Montaigne realizes that it is easier to judge, to experience physical phenomena. Nevertheless, one surmises that therein lies the germ and origin of his belief in judgment's capacity to sift, among all the tests and experiences which the self undergoes, his true psychological and moral being, on the basis of the intimate and material knowledge which judgment has of it.

Montaigne's concern for the self-reliance and self-experience of judgment is particularly evident in his quest for sound health and the physical as well as psychological well-being and contentment which it entails. As he states in "Que le goust des biens et des maux depend en bonne partie de l'opinion que nous en avons," man's ills, physical or psychosomatic and psychological, are often the product of reason, of a judgment that has not experienced the material phenomena. The non-intellectual facet of life must not be reasoned and intellectualized. The role of judgment is to remain "disponible," in a constant state of readiness, able to judge the actual and material experience as it occurs, and not dissipate and lose itself in vain anticipation. It is for this reason that Montaigne dislikes medicine and scorns the vast majority of its practitioners. They thrive on man's imagination and dilute and delude his ability to experience and judge for himself. In "De l'experience," Montaigne describes the inner turmoil which medicine activated in his judgment, that is his sense and awareness of what is right or wrong for his own being:

> Je n'en estois abbatu ny deslogé de ma place, mais j'en estois heurté et poussé; si mon jugement n'en est ny changé ny troublé, au moins il en estoit empesché; c'est tousjours agitation et combat (III, 13, 1068).

Judgment guides man in the present, in and through his physical, psychological, and moral being as it creates and identifies itself by means of unadulterated "épreuves" or experiences.

The faculty of judgment does not concern itself only with the analysis of personal experience. Judgment comes into being through experience, through an indefinite series of "essais." Judgment is the sum and substance of personal experience; to judge implies the creation of identity for the experienced phenomena and for judgment itself.

Occasionally, Montaigne goes beyond merely suggesting the need of material experience in order to enhance the accuracy and effectiveness of judgment. In several cases, he states categorically that one cannot fathom the sorrows of others by judgment alone. Physical presence and the knowledge acquired, felt by the senses, that is visual and auditory perception as well as that which lodges itself in the heart, are essential and immeasurable facets of true judgment:

> nulle sagesse ne va si avant de concevoir la cause d'une tristesse si vive et entiere par jugement, qu'elle ne souffre accession par la presence, quand les yeux et les oreilles y ont part, parties qui ne peuvent estre agitées que par vains accidens (III, 4, 815).

Man's understanding is enhanced through actual presence, through material experience. There is no substitute for knowledge which can be immediately perceived and felt. In "De l'exercitation," Montaigne experiences what, for him, proves to be the most accurate acquaintance of death which one can obtain. On the basis of his fall from a horse, Montaigne surmises that reason and education in and of themselves do not suffice. Experience, that is the actual participation of one's being, is an essential element in the search for knowledge.[1] As Montaigne describes its formation and acquisition in "De l'institution des enfans," the faculty of judgment is the product of all three.

Because accuracy of knowledge is the goal which Montaigne sets for judgment, the subject of personal experience involves a question of general validity. In other words, is there a possibility of universalizing the individual experience? For that matter, is Montaigne concerned with the systematization of experience? That he is aware of the problem caused by the disparity of experiences is as evident in "De la ressemblance des enfans aux peres" as it is in "De l'experience." Few people bother to record their experiences and more importantly the possibility of contrary experiences is extensive.[2]

Lanson states that Montaigne sees the solution to the problem of differing experiences in the organization of experience: "La recherche des effets de la nature qui peuvent servir à l'homme, est un art, elle doit

[1] II, 6, 350.
[2] II, 37, 763.

être 'réglée et méthodique.' Il faut inventer des moyens de s'assurer si ce qu'on prend pour la cause est bien cause." [1] There is perhaps a tendency to extend the meaning of *organiser* to include the preparation and organization of an experiment; this would be contrary to Montaigne's conception of judgment and experience. The term *organiser* applies only if it is intended to mean that Montaigne wants to assemble, to reorganize that which was experienced. Montaigne seeks to understand, to penetrate experience in order to apprehend causality. He records, sifts, and discerns, but he neither prepares nor organizes experiments.

As Montaigne states in "De l'art de conferer," the fruit of experience is the acquisition of means with which to form one's judgment. Physicians, for example, must assimilate individual experience in order that their judgment be better equipped to diagnose medical problems which may arise in the future. Judgment is the synthesis of individual analyses; judgment is assimilated, organic experience: "Ce n'est pas assez de compter les experiences, il les faut poiser et assortir et les faut avoir digerées et alambiquées, pour en tirer les raisons et conclusions qu'elles portent" (III, 8, 909). It is in the sense of *poiser, assortir, digérer,* and *alambiquer* (to distill) that one may speak of a systematized, experimental, method in Montaigne's conception of judgment and experience. Montaigne does not seek to build logical demonstrations but to analyze.

Generally, Montaigne finds that there are no universals, no essences. The diversity of essential alteration can only be resolved within one's being. The terms *system, systematic, systematize* do not apply to Montaigne, because he believes that the varieties of human experience refute all systems. It is for this reason that Montaigne prefers experience in all of its complex variety to any rigid notion of essence. Judgment, the existential experience, is an open-ended, unbounded and limitless entity.

In the coalition of judgment and experience, Montaigne relies on an innate sense of what is true or false, good or evil. At times, his judgment is the product of a strong, personal feeling or experience; frequently, it is the result of a somewhat more concrete sensation or experience. In "De la cruauté," he contends that he can maintain his judgment and his immoral inclinations as separate entities. The Stoics argue that man functions as a whole; if he is being virtuous, all his virtues assist him. Montaigne opposes the Stoics on the grounds that they may conse-

[1] Lanson, *Les Essais de Montaigne*, p. 279.

quently infer that a man who sins is propelled simultaneously by all his vices: "je ne les en croy pas ainsi simplement, ou je ne les entens pas, car je sens par effect le contraire" (II, 11, 408). Montaigne senses the contrary of the stoical proposition within himself; he deems his immediate feeling or apprehension to be superior to their philosophical reasoning. He contradicts principles and authority on the basis of an intuitive and unverifiable feeling. This inexplicable, non-intellectual aspect of Montaigne's judgment is the product of intimate and personal experience and knowledge of the self.

Moore finds that in the sixteenth century the term *experience* described something "felt or perceived in an immediate and lively way ... It is opposed to what is apprehended by the mind." [1] Montaigne's frequent use of the verb *sentir* characterizes the concrete, "experienced," aspect of judgment and experience. In "Des livres," Montaigne deplores Cicero's poetry and more importantly his inability to recognize, to feel, that is to experience intimately, to judge accurately, the ineptness of his poetry in light of his reputation: "ce n'est pas grande imperfection que de mal faire des vers; mais c'est à luy faute de jugement de n'avoir pas senty combien ils estoyent indignes de la gloire de son nom" (II, 10, 395). To some degree, when one recalls the juxtaposition of man and animals in the "Apologie," judgment, that is the innate feeling of truth and falsehood, good and evil, is to man as instinct is to animals. There is a definite intuitive and instinctive aspect to judgment which leads Montaigne to rely increasingly on experience, on the personal feeling and sensation.

In "De la phisionomie," Montaigne declares: "[je] ne suis pas homme qui me laisse guiere garroter le jugement par preoccupation" (III, 11, 1010). The opportunity to question and converse with a dozen condemned witches prompts him to judge that they are more deserving of a fool's antidote than of hemlock. Montaigne insists on personal confrontation, participation, experience. The critical faculty of judgment must see and decide for itself; judgment depends upon experience, the immediate "épreuve" of phenomena. As in the case of his opposition to a stoical point of view, all abstract principles and all preconceptions wane in the light of intimate experience. The notion of "essai," "essayer," that is to experience,[2] is not only the role and primary activity of judgment; it is also the verification and concreti-

[1] Moore, p. 41.

[2] For a detailed study of this question, see S. Hamel, "*Experience-Essai.* Contribution à l'étude du vocabulaire de Montaigne," *BSAM*, 11–12 (1959), 23–32.

zation of a highly sound and sensitive judgment. Judgment and experience coalesce in Montaigne's "essai" of death: "Or, à présent que je l'ay essayé par effect, je ne fay nul doubte que je n'en aye bien jugé jusques à cette heure" (II, 6, 355).

Experimental judgment supersedes objective knowledge. Montaigne's critical intelligence and sense, perhaps his greatest quality, exercises itself within the realm of the subjective. Subjectively, that is "experimentally," man's judgment can only attain and formulate approximations of his being and of his knowledge. Nevertheless, this knowledge of the self and of others is more intense and accurate because it is deeply felt. In the study of the self and of others, man's judgment experiences, that is judges. Quite literally, to judge, to activate into being, means to experience. Montaigne formulates an incomparable synthesis of this aspect of the notion of judgment and experience in "De l'amitié." On the subject of friendship, he would prefer speaking to someone who might have "essayé" what he is discussing. However, the scarcity of a friendship like his leads him to believe that it will not be properly known and understood:

> je ne m'attens pas d'en trouver aucun bon juge. Car les discours mesmes que l'antiquité nous a laissé sur ce subject me semblent lâches au prix du sentiment que j'en ay. Et, en ce poinct, les effects surpassent les preceptes mesmes de la philosophie (I, 28, 191–192).

In "De l'experience," Montaigne discusses at length the properties of experience as opposed to those of reason. His primary concern throughout the essay is the state of his health; he attempts to depict his knowledge of the "ressorts de Nature" within him which control his health and enable him to be as "naturally" happy and content as he can be. Because his health is so much a part of his thought, the practice of medicine is constantly attacked for what it is, an act of divination with no basis in fact, an art of intimidating the unsuspecting and unknowledgeable patient, a field which includes a great deal of unintelligible language but scant learning and experience.

Montaigne emphasizes the superiority of fact over anticipation, of experience over reason, of judgment over imagination. The feeling that something is perhaps crumbling in his body does not compel him to test his pulse and his urine in order to circumvent some unknown occurrence. The pain which he will experience when it happens will be sufficient. Montaigne does not plan on suffering "imaginatively": "Je ne me juge que par vray sentiment, non par discours" (III, 13, 1074). Montaigne assesses the state of his health as he feels it in its presentness.

Judgment does not theorize; it experiences. One recalls Montaigne's frequent use of *tâter*, *toucher*, and *goûter*. Judgment's knowledge of physical, intellectual, psychological, and moral phenomena is certain and indubitable.

Although Montaigne is referring to the physical aspect of his being, to his sensitivity to pain, it is by means of the "interne attouchement," as he calls it in the "Apologie" (II, 12, 571), that he defines the role of judgment in its constant analysis of the self. Montaigne judges his being in action, in experience, not hypothetically nor experimentally. There are actual and true reverberations of being which the faculty of judgment experiences. The function of judgment is to analyze the self in its reality, in the experience, in the solid and concrete "épreuve" which it has of the self. Judgment operates in the realm of fact; its primary occupation is the separation of fact from fiction, the establishment of appearance and reality.

Judgment and experience, that is "épreuve," "essai," comprise extensive and extended being. The interaction and frequent interdependency of judgment and experience are not to be considered as momentary phases in the analysis of the self. Because Montaigne judges in order to build for the future, the record which the faculty of judgment makes of present experience must act as a guide to future action and behavior. Self-experience and self-judgment must attain truth, that is the truth of happiness. The role of judgment becomes the formation and guidance of a productive, useful, self-satisfying, and happy existence. The whole of life is the test of judgment.

THE RELATIONSHIP OF JUDGMENT AND LIFE

Montaigne is particularly proud of his faculty of judgment. He senses that he owes it the well-being of his physical and psychological personality. Moreover, he knows that the *Essais* which he is writing are the children, the emanations and offshoots, of his judgment. More importantly, Montaigne recognizes that judgment, that is his judgment and that of man in general, is one of the most important subjects of the *Essais*.

Accordingly, Montaigne occasionally remarks that the *Essais* are the products of his natural faculties. More specifically, he reminds the reader that he is promulgating the "essais" of his judgment. In "De Democritus et Heraclitus," he remarks that he "essays," that is tries and tests his judgment whenever he can: "Le jugement est un util à tous subjects, et se mesle par tout. A cette cause, aux essais que j'en fay ici, j'y employe toute sorte d'occasion" (I, 50, 289). In this example, there is no doubt that Montaigne is engaged in presenting his personal opinions, in judging by himself. The object of his judgment's scrutiny consists of various and sundry subjects.

On the other hand, the composition of "De la praesumption" (1578–1580) reflects the emergence of a unique, personal, and viable subject, that is Montaigne's judgment, a psychological and moral representation of himself, a fit subject for study. The knowledge which others may gain of his personality is inured by the "essais" of his judgment:

quel que je me face connoistre, pourveu que je me face connoistre tel que je suis, je fay mon effect .... sans l'advertissement d'autruy, je voy assez ce peu que tout cecy vaut et poise, et la folie de mon dessein. C'est prou que mon jugement ne se defferre poinct, duquel ce sont icy les essais (II, 17, 636–637).

The "je," the observer, and the "me," the observed, fuse into one demonstrable and recognizable entity, that is Montaigne's judgment. The sequential progression in the previous lines indicates that it is judgment which is to be made known. Montaigne's disparate essence and duality of being are unified within judgment.

Montaigne or his judgment is to be made known by means of "essais"; *connoistre* is the end of *essais* as *jugement* is that of *je* and *me*. The term *essai*, by its very nature, connotes a serial, that is a plural, production. Montaigne knows that he cannot place himself in the center of the stage as a ready-made object. Hence, Montaigne conceives of himself, of his judgment, as a serialized or ever-unfolding entity. As Montaigne's vision of human nature distends and broadens, the faculty of judgment, that is man's identity and personality, is seen to represent the individual's organic, serialized, unfolding, and all-inclusive journey through life. The "essais" are no longer the trials of judgment but the tests, the experiences of life: "En fin, toute cette fricassée que je barbouille icy n'est qu'un registre des essais de ma vie" (III, 13, 1056). Judgment becomes the embodiment of the entire man, a life in time and space.

The expanding scope and significance of the concept of judgment, its literal progression from *jugement* to *vie*, is particularly evident in the textual revisions of "De l'institution des enfans." In the 1580 edition of the *Essais*, Montaigne insisted that the preceptor assess the child's judgment:

Qu'il ne luy demande pas seulement compte des mots de sa leçon, mais du sens et de la substance, et qu'il juge du profit qu'il aura fait, non par le tesmoignage de sa memoire, mais de son jugement (I, 26, 149).

The term *jugement* remained in the successive 1582, 1587, and 1588 editions. It was in the course of his post-1588 additions and corrections that Montaigne changed *jugement* to *vie*. The substitution of *vie* for *jugement* reinforces the notion that the proper statement of Montaigne's subject is to be found in "De l'experience" and not in "De Democritus et Heraclitus" or in "De la praesumption." For Montaigne, the *Essais* are the record of his life's experiences, as he experienced, witnessed, and analyzed them.

Michaut, in his critical edition of "De l'institution des enfans," remarks that Montaigne strengthens the import of his thought by substituting *vie* for *jugement*. He argues that it might be difficult to verify the probity of man's judgment, for it could manifest itself by mere words, that is the regurgitation of a memorized lesson. By substituting *vie* for *jugement*, Montaigne infers that man must be judged by his acts, by his life, and not by words alone.[1] To be sure, Montaigne thinks in terms of judging personality as it manifests itself in action. However, action is being, the source and the product of judgment, and the substitution of terms is a clarification of the evolution which the organic and spatial structure of the notion of judgment has undergone in Montaigne's mind.

On the other hand, Lanson sees the progression of Montaigne's stated purpose from tests of judgment to experiences of life as the objectification of a formerly subjective endeavor. Lanson contends that, for Montaigne, it is no longer a question of testing himself, but rather one of experiencing things, life.[2] On the contrary, the whole of life remains, for Montaigne, a field of subjective study. His notion of experience and judgment indicates that his knowledge of the world about him is obtained through his physical and psychological being, as it experiences outside phenomena. Montaigne clearly emphasizes that the *Essais* are a record of *his* life, not of life in general.

Montaigne's progression from judgment to life is neither a dissipation of self, nor a depersonalization. It is an amplification of judgment, an awareness of the continuity of judgment. Montaigne's judgment is *what it has become*, a life. The concept of life is the only one capable of energizing and validating judgment's inherent state of subjective and adaptable becomingness. Judgment is the sum and substance of *a* life, an accumulation of "experienced" judgments, a personality. Brunetière has aptly remarked that Montaigne's definition of life might be "adap-

[1] G. Michaut, ed. *De l'institution des enfants* (Paris, 1924), p. 19, n. 32.
[2] Lanson, *Les Essais de Montaigne*, p. 112, no. 80.

tation," for our personality, "si nous en avons une, ne se dégagera que de ce conflit de tous les jours avec les circonstances. On ne naît pas 'soi-même,' ... on le devient!" [1] Montaigne spent his life seeking himself; his especial pleasure and discovery was the knowledge that his judgment was both the seeker and the material sought. Following the dictum "know thyself," Montaigne finds himself in his lifetime.

[1] Ferdinand Brunetière, "Publications récentes sur Montaigne," *Revue des deux mondes*, XXXV (1906), 215.

CHAPTER IV

THE RELATIONSHIP OF JUDGMENT TO THE OTHER FACULTIES

"Les *Essais* sont un livre déconcertant et mystérieux." [1]

In the study of the concept of judgment in Montaigne, one encounters an exciting but perplexing and disconcerting problem of related vocabulary. Montaigne's acute attentiveness to the activities of the mind often leads him to employ freely several terms which closely parallel the ideational connotations of the concept of judgment in the sixteenth-century and in his work. The terms *jugement, entendement, sens, raison, discours*, and *conscience* form a semantic field which enables Montaigne not only to vary his vocabulary but also to establish graded differences among the words. In general this study discusses the notion of judgment throughout the *Essais* and in Montaigne's other works. The purpose of this chapter is to examine briefly five related psychological terms and to discuss the problem of their relationship to the faculty of judgment.

A statistical analysis of the frequency distribution and chronology of the occurrences of these psychological terms reveals little or no information which might not be obtained by other means. The word *raison* is the predominant term primarily because of its frequent appearances in the "Apologie de Raimond Sebond." When one links *raison* to the term *discours*, its closest ideational ally, one finds that their combined usage nearly doubles the occurrence of *jugement*, which appears 212 times in the *Essais*. A purely distributional and statistical approach would lead one to believe that Montaigne places greater stress on the deficiencies than on the possibilities of man's mind, for the term *raison* is more often than not presented pejoratively.

Furthermore, one finds no noticeable difference in the chronological strata of the various terms. The word *entendement* preserves the same connotations after 1588 as it did prior to 1580. Throughout his production of the *Essais*, Montaigne consistently considers *jugement* to be superior to the other psychological terms. However, he continues

[1] Fortunat Strowski, *La Sagesse française* (Paris, 1925), p. 75.

occasionally to use *jugement* pejoratively after 1588 as he did during the composition of the "Apologie de Raimond Sebond."

It cannot be said that Montaigne maintains a high degree of fixed parallelism within his use of a psychological term and its referential object or topic. Yet, in "De l'institution des enfans," an essay which of necessity bears heavily on the importance and training of the mind and in which terms that describe various possible activities of the mind are plentiful, Montaigne sparingly uses *raison* and *sens* (two times each) and gives the advantage to *jugement* (14 times) and *entendement* (11 times). Throughout this essay, *jugement* and *entendement* seem to be synonymous; *jugement* constitutes a superior mental and moral possibility which Montaigne wishes to attain, train, and enhance. Although Montaigne at times equates *raison*, *sens*, and *jugement*, one might say that his utilization of *raison*, and particularly of *sens*, is minimal in "De l'institution des enfans," because he recognizes that *sens* is not a faculty which can be trained. The productions of *sens* may equal those of *jugement*, but its existence as an asset and faculty comes into being by other means. Hence, *jugement* and *sens*, while frequently identical, are not synonymous on all topical levels.

Within Montaigne's ideational revelation of himself and of his thought, certain terms may, at a given moment in time and with reference to a particular topic, reveal new possibilities and present new or different meanings. However, semantically speaking, these terms never change. The ideational synonymity or divergence and the connections which exist between these psychological terms are never clearly stated, perhaps because Montaigne's roving and associative mind compels him to see the flow and continuity of things; abrupt and well-defined demarcation lines do not interest him nor do they appear feasible.

Occasionally, Montaigne seems to make distinctions in his use of these terms, but the ensuing connections which one is bound to establish and interpret may not necessarily exist. Montaigne frequently repeats himself; certain phrases, patterns of words, and parallel structures reappear before his mind's eye and seem automatically to impose themselves upon his thought. He often associates one word with another, and the use of the first term recalls the second. In other words, Montaigne favors certain phrases and combinations of words which hinder a classification of verbally presented psychological relationships. It is certain that there exist subtle but frequently ill-defined nuances in his use of psychological terms. It is also true that he repeatedly employs some of these words as synonyms. There are instances in which Montaigne seems to use his psychological terms with abandon. It is for this reason that the specific context rather than a general view is the only key to an understanding of these terms and of their relationship.

In general, Montaigne remains within the accepted confines of the vocabulary of his century. Rather than invent new words, he gives new meanings and significance to terms already in existence by stressing their Latin origin. Without creating new vehicles of expression, he greatly expands and enlarges the semantic possibilities of his lexicon; one need only unearth the Latin etymon of a particular word in order to gain a fuller understanding of Montaigne's meaning. However, in the case of terms which denote a specific activity of the mind, Montaigne tends to use these words according to their general acceptation.

ENTENDEMENT

The term *entendement* (understanding) seems to be the fundamental word for the description of mental activity; precisely, without *entendement* one does not function mentally. Although Montaigne consistently retains this basic meaning (he never considers the emotional aspects of *entendement*), he enlarges it by equating it with other terms, particularly *jugement.*

In the sixteenth century, the faculty of understanding (*entendement*) is habitually the ability to understand and comprehend;[1] it is the mental faculty which enables one to know, both in the sense of *connaître* and of *savoir.* Of all the expressions which can describe activities of the mind, *entendement* has the broadest applications, for its primary meaning is intelligence.[2]

Entendement embodies all the discursive possibilities of the mind; it conceives, it reasons, and it judges. Malebranche defines *entendement* or the faculty of understanding by opposing it to sensations: "par ce mot, *entendement pur,* nous ne prétendons désigner que la faculté qu'a l'esprit de connoître les objets de dehors sans qu'il s'en forme des images corporelles dans le cerveau pour les représenter." [3] It is feasible

[1] Hatzfeld and Darmesteter, I, 914; Godefroy, IX, 481.

[2] Henri Taine, in the prologue to his tract on *De l'intelligence,* 13th ed. (Paris, 1914), I, i, states that "si je ne me trompe, on entend aujourd'hui par intelligence ce qu'on entendait autrefois par entendement ou intellect, à savoir la faculté de connaître; du moins, j'ai pris le mot dans ce sens."

[3] Malebranche, *Recherche de la vérité,* ed. Geneviève Rodis-Lewis in *Œuvres complètes* (Paris, 1958–1965), I, 381. Although a seventeenth-century writer and philosopher, his definition of *entendement* is also applicable to the sixteenth century in the same way that the

to assume that for Montaigne and his contemporaries there exists an underlying antithesis between understanding and reason.[1] While both faculties share equally in the pursuit and acquisition of knowledge, *entendement* is a form of direct knowledge or intuition as opposed to reason, the faculty which enables one to know discursively. For Montaigne, *entendement* always means intelligence [2] or intellect and particularly the sound and masterly use of intellect. In "De l'inconstance de nos actions," Montaigne remarks that "ce n'est pas tour de rassis entendement de nous juger simplement par nos actions de dehors" (II, 1, 321). Montaigne implies that it is unintelligent and unwise to judge a book by its cover; to abandon the interior for the surface is the accomplishment of a poor intellect.

Throughout the *Essais*, Montaigne repeatedly uses the term *entendement* as a qualifying epithet. Whenever he wants to bestow praise or show his admiration for a man's thought and deeds, he speaks of an "homme d'entendement," of a "seigneur de bon entendement," or of "gens d'entendement." For Montaigne, the appellation "homme d'entendement" describes the highest quality that can be attributed to a man. Because of his utilization of the term in these constructions, *entendement* is as much a quality as it is a faculty. It is no longer basic intelligence, but rather applied intelligence which is employed and channelled in a manner which appeals to Montaigne. As a quality, *entendement* is usually interchangeable with *jugement*, the cultivated ability of discerning the truth or falsehood of new appearances. However, the moral aspect frequently associated with *jugement* is not always an intrinsic part of *entendement*, as the treatment of conscience will tend to demonstrate.

Montaigne seldom attaches pejorative signification to *entendement*; there are no more than a dozen such occurrences. His sarcasm and irony toward *entendement* never attain the withering effectiveness which is unleashed on *raison*, *discours*, and frequently *jugement*. When *entendement* appears by itself as a faculty and when it is used as a qualifier, Montaigne's intent is a benevolent one; the faculty of *entendement* should be a highly esteemed possession. It is only when he adds *humain*,

Dictionnaire de l'Académie française, published 20 years later in 1694, is frequently referred to as a substantially accurate compendium of late sixteenth-century terminology.

[1] A distinction between the understanding as *ratio* and the understanding as *intellectus* is drawn by the Middle Ages: see Josef Pieper, *Leisure: The Basis of Culture* (New York, 1952), pp. 11–12 and Henri Vernay, *Les Divers Sens du mot raison autour de l'œuvre de Marguerite d'Angoulême Reine de Navarre (1492–1549)* (Heidelberg), 1962, p. 93.

[2] Villey in *Les Essais de Michel de Montaigne*, ed. Fortunat Strowski *et al.* (Bordeaux, 1906–1933), V, 251.

as in *l'entendement humain*, that he takes it to task and derides it;[1] in these instances, he tends to equate *entendement* with the pejorative applications of *raison*.[2]

It is interesting to note that Montaigne never describes a man as an "homme de jugement." Yet, the phrase is used in the sixteenth century: "Tout homme de jugement comprendra assés quelle est la suffisance et habileté de son entendouere loiolitique."[3] Initially, and perhaps throughout the progression of his thought, Montaigne associates *entendement* with superior human beings. He particularly applies it to the sages of antiquity and those of his period, especially La Boétie, whom he wishes to emulate in spirit and in deed: "The man he admires is the learned sage whom he calls 'the man of understanding'."[4] In "De la coustume et de ne changer aisément une loy receuë," Montaigne characterizes the man of understanding as one who has achieved complete mastery of his person.[5] The sage or the "homme d'entendement" is an intelligent and prudent man whom Montaigne customarily opposes to the "vulgaire."

To a certain extent, when *entendement* is used as an epithet, it contains a societal, stratified connotation as well as a mental one. It constitutes an almost social and intellectual category. In discussing La Boétie's *La Servitude volontaire*, he remarks that the pamphlet "court pieça és mains des gens d'entendement, non sans bien grande et méritée recommandation: car il est gentil, et plein ce qu'il est possible" (I, 28, 182). It is difficult to visualize the tract in the hands of anyone else. The "gens d'entendement" consist of a class of well-educated, well-bred, and lettered men who find themselves in positions of power, influence, affluence, and leisure, and whose interests include political theory.

Moreover, Montaigne tends to associate a lowly station in life with

[1] II, 12, 538–539: "ce n'est pas merveille si, en chose si haute et ancienne, l'entendement humain se trouble et dissipe." II, 12, 538: "l'entendement humain se perd[ant] à vouloir sonder et contreroller toutes choses jusques au bout." In these examples, and in many others, *entendement* signifies intellect, intelligence, and frequently mind as opposed to body; the latter instance occurs in "Contre la faineantise," II, 21, 660: "ce fut aussi le seul office de Capitaine qu'il resigna; tous les autres, necessaires et utiles, il les fit très-laborieusement et exactement; tenant son corps couché, mais son entendement et son courage debout et ferme, jusques au dernier, et aucunement au delà."

[2] On the subject of frivolous adaptability, he identifies *entendement* with *raison* to such an extent that one is immediately struck by a feeling of *déjà vu*, both in terms of idea and vocabulary: "Il n'est rien si soupple et erratique que nostre entendement; c'est le soulier de Theramenez, bon à tous pieds. Et il est double et divers et les matieres doubles et diverses" (III, 11, 1012).

[3] Philippe de Marnix, *Tableau des différends de la religion* in *Œuvres de Philippe de Marnix de Sainte Aldegonde*, ed. Albert Lacroix (Brussels, 1857–1860), I, 6.

[4] Frame, *Montaigne's Discovery of Man*, p. 45.

[5] I, 23, 117.

a low caliber of *entendement*. Aware that a beggar is often happier than he, Montaigne resolves to attain the same level of patience and habit through reasoning and intellectual examination, for "ne puis croire que la bassesse de l'entendement puisse plus que la vigueur" (I, 39, 238). Montaigne automatically ascribes less intellectual vigor, finesse, and ingenuity to the beggar. Perhaps Montaigne intends to distinguish between a reason which is exercised and one which remains dormant, between an educated man and an illiterate mendicant. To say the least, this association of mind and social position strikes an ambivalent chord in Montaigne's notion of unadulterated intelligence and education or culture.

In the "Apologie de Raimond Sebond," Montaigne reproves the capacity of reason to rationalize the soundness of all modes of thought:

> Mais ce, qu'il ne se void aucune proposition qui ne soit debatue et controverse entre nous, ou qui ne le puisse estre, montre bien que nostre jugement naturel ne saisit pas bien clairement ce qu'il saisit. Car mon jugement ne le peut faire recevoir au jugement de mon compaignon (II, 12, 545).

It seems that Montaigne qualifies judgment as "naturel" when it is a matter of discussing something which should be equally clear to all men. The adjective "naturel" expands the applicability of *jugement* and modifies it as a common denominator or attribute. In "De l'institution des enfans," Montaigne remarks that his lack of "science" requires him to test the child's "jugement naturel," that is his personal intellectual prowess which is devoid of facts, figures, and information. In both cases, Montaigne alludes to intellect or native intelligence, that is *entendement*. Montaigne never describes *entendement* as "naturel"; its essence is that it be "naturel." Conversely, whenever Montaigne adds "naturel" to *jugement*, the context is always one in which *entendement* appears to be the more appropriate term. One can only conclude that Montaigne is referring to *entendement*, basic intelligence, when he employs *jugement naturel*.

Another pattern of lexical qualification which tends to erect a distinction between *entendement* and *jugement* is found within the various verbs which Montaigne chooses to accompany the term *entendement*. In general, these verbs are verbs of action and they particularly connote incipient action. They are well chosen to underline and depict the conception and conceptualization of ideas which is the primary function of *entendement*. These verbs are usually *venir à*, *tomber en*, *recevoir en*, *entrer en*, and *se présenter à*.[1] *Entendement* is the

[1] Montaigne asks La Boétie to relate all his ideas and opinions: "Il ne fut jamais, suyvis-je,

seat of man's intellectual activity; all mental processes are engendered within *entendement.* It is for this reason that Montaigne can quickly bound from *jugement* to *entendement,* since *jugement* must be an aspect of *entendement.* Indeed, Van den Bruwaene suspects that *jugement* is a virtue, a quality, and that *entendement* refers to the intellectual faculty which can possess it.[1] Therefore, it is not inconceivable that Montaigne could transpose one for the other while still retaining an underlying distinction.

The essay "De l'institution des enfans" demonstrates the degree of complexity involved in the stratification and relationships of *entendement, sens,* and *jugement.* Montaigne insists upon the formation of character and judgment. Indeed, character (*meurs*) remains a fixed constant to which Montaigne adds one faculty after another. He asks that the child's preceptor have "plutost la teste bien faicte que bien pleine, et qu'on y requit tous les deux, mais plus les meurs et l'entendement que la science" (I, 26, 149). In this instance, *entendement* represents the quality or faculty which Montaigne advocates, that is *jugement,* and which he constantly opposes to "science." On the other hand, in the course of enumerating the means by which to form judgment, he remarks that to his mind "les premiers discours dequoy on luy doit abreuver l'entendement, ce doivent estre ceux qui reglent ses meurs et son sens" (I, 26, 158). A significant semantic shift has taken place; in the first example, *entendement* is a highly prized mental attribute which is to be sought. In the second passage, *entendement* is assumed; the child possesses it, that is a mind, and it is to be instructed. It is only because of *meurs* that *entendement* in the first quotation and *sens* in the second become momentarily synonymous and interchangeable, for in

que je n'eusse cest honneur que de communiquer à toutes celles qui vous venoient à l'entendement, voulez-vous pas que j'en jouisse encore?," "Fragment d'une lettre," *Œuvres complètes,* ed. Albert Thibaudet and Maurice Rat (Paris, 1962), p. 1358. In the same letter, pp. 1355–1356, Montaigne recounts La Boétie's admonitions to his niece: "Je ne vous deffens pas le vice qui est tant detestable aux femmes: car je ne veux pas penser seulement, qu'il vous puisse tomber en l'entendement." The *Essais* contain all the variations: "Il nous devroit souvenir, quoy que nous receussions en l'entendement, que nous y recevons souvent des choses fauces, et que c'est par ces mesmes utils qui se démentent et qui se trompent souvent" (II, 12, 546–547). In this example, *entendement* and *jugement* are greatly at variance since *jugement* is one of the tools which informs *entendement* and enables it to understand the truth. Montaigne deplores a concept of virtue based on the desirability of public honor, "un' opinion si fauce que je suis dépit qu'elle ait jamais peu entrer en l'entendement d'homme qui eust cet honneur de porter le nom de philosophe" (II, 16, 604). Money makes a lawyer see a case in its true light: "Voilà une apparente et indubitable verité qui se presente à son entendement" (II, 12, 550).

[1] Léon Van den Bruwaene, "Les Idées philosophiques de Montaigne," *Revue néo-scolastique de philosophie,* XXXV (1933), 505.

the second example, in which both terms appear concomitantly, they are diametrically opposed: *entendement* acquires *sens.*

Considered separately, these psychological terms seem to retain an individual identity; one thinks they embrace a meaning which perhaps is not found in the other words. When they are brought together, their admittedly slight variations enter into synonymity by virtue of another term or concept which ushers them into Montaigne's consciousness. The notions of virtue and "science" or memory are two other words which bring about synonymity. Virtue, as *meurs*, summons forth an interchangeable complementary term, whereas "science" creates equality within the psychological terms because of Montaigne's unerring antithetical mode of thought. Since Montaigne is more apt to couple *entendement* or *sens* with *meurs*, and since, at times, he seems to take *jugement* to mean character, one wonders if the composite or end product of *meurs* and *entendement* or *meurs* and *sens* is not indeed *jugement.*

The problem of relationships is further complicated by the fact that Montaigne occasionally indulges in the Rabelaisian characteristic of accumulation and congestion. In "De la ressemblance des enfans aux peres," he revels in one of his many attacks on medicine. Like Pericles, he believes that the best way to answer questions concerning the state of one's health is to point to the medications which one is taking:

> "Vous le pouvez juger par là," montrant ma main chargée de six dragmes d'opiate: ce sera un bien evident signe d'une maladie violente. J'auray mon jugement merveilleusement desmanché; si l'impatience et la frayeur gaignent cela sur moy, on en pourra conclurre une bien aspre fiévre en mon ame (II, 37, 765–766).

As it stands, this passage presents no difficulty. Judgment, his capacity to discern and understand things in their true light, bears the mark of an insensible and emotional upheaval. However, all editions through 1588 contained after the word *violente* "et qui ara troublé l'assiette de mon entendement et de ma raison." *Entendement, raison,* and *jugement* are all susceptible to disturbances but they need not all be represented. In this illustration, there is no apparent gradation among them. These three terms appear to be synonymous, and it is probably for this reason that Montaigne omits *entendement* and *raison* after 1588. The fact that he initially brought them together can perhaps be attributed to an unconscious desire to portray forcefully and emphatically the extent and ramifications of medecine's effect upon the unwary individual.

A considerably more basic and seemingly fundamental distinction is destroyed, ignored, or overlooked in two separate comparisons of Frenchmen and Italians. In "De la vanité des paroles," Montaigne agrees with "les Italiens, qui se vantent, et avecques raison, d'avoir communément l'esprit plus esveillé et le discours plus sain que les autres nations de leur temps" (I, 51, 295). Later, in "De l'art de conferer," he deplores the loss or lack of an art of discussion in France. The Athenians and the Romans maintained this rewarding exercise in their Academies, and "de nostre temps, les Italiens en retiennent quelques vestiges, à leur grand profict, comme il se voit par la comparaison de nos entendemens aux leurs" (III, 8, 900). Montaigne usually considers *esprit* and *entendement* as two independent entities; *esprit* is the more garrulous, frivolous, and unstable of the two, while *entendement*, in the sense of *jugement*, is preferred. However, *entendement* or *jugement* need not necessarily ignore *esprit*; it can often learn from *esprit*, for if it can harness its boundless energy and curiosity, it can substantially increase the effectiveness of its own performance. *Jugement* and *sens* are normally associated with *entendement* whereas *raison* and *discours* rotate within the enclave of *esprit*. In the preceding passages, *entendement* and *esprit* are synonymous, a rather rare occurrence in Montaigne's vocabulary. Separated in time, two passages treating an identical idea have elicited two supposedly distinct terms. It can be seen that the fluidity and adaptability of the language combine with Montaigne's insouciant inconsistency to make the formulation and articulation of reasonably hard and fast definitions a delicate enterprise.

Montaigne interchanges his psychological terms with such ease that one is frequently compelled to equate them. It is nearly impossible to determine the differences, if any, between one word and another when he brings them together as he does, for example, in "De l'institution des enfans." Indeed, *jugement* and *entendement* are bound to conflict in Montaigne's mind; they are too closely associated. Even their syllabic structure and sound pattern seem to invite one to amalgamate them. Although Montaigne remains conscious of certain disagreements among these two terms, he is not always able to disentangle and identify them. His awareness of these incongruities can be seen in certain lexical patterns which he combines with specific terms. Nevertheless, as has been noted, these patterns are also capable of obscuring as well as elucidating and clarifying an analysis of the relationships which Montaigne presents.

In general, *entendement* tends to remain strongly associated with the idea of intelligence, intellect, and occasionally the brain. In fact, it is often misused for reason. Its basic ability or charge is that of conception rather than criticism. It is used incidentally as the equivalent of *jugement*, whose intellectual role has been depicted as the ability to encounter new appearances and determine their relative degree of truth and falsehood. It is in this sense that Montaigne uses *entendement* in the following lines:

après que, selon vostre bel entendement, vous avez estably les limites de la verité et de la mensonge ... vous vous estez desjà obligé de les abandonner (I, 27, 180).

Frequently, *entendement* equals *jugement* because Montaigne is examining antithetically a few favorite targets of his ire, such as memory. He conceives of *entendement* as an intellectual capability whereas *jugement* is a quality which is obtained through the mutual checks and balances of a man's intellectual, moral, psychological, and social existence. Judgment is wisdom; *entendement* or intelligence need not be.

SENS

Wisdom, in the broadest sense of the term, is best depicted by *sens*, the most problematic of the psychological words which Montaigne uses because he and his contemporaries have a tendency to use it as an all-purpose term. *Sens* can span an intellectual area ranging between its aspects as a common denominator of humanity and the highest possibilities of *jugement*.

Writers in the sixteenth century seem to equate *sens* with *jugement* more readily than with *entendement*. They particularly attribute to *sens* the possibility of making distinctions between truth and falsehood rather than the power of conception.[1]

Nevertheless, Robert Estienne describes Latin *mens* as *sens* and *entendement*, and Nicot states that the loss of one's senses is rendered jointly in French by *sens* and *entendement*.[2] Hence, it can be seen that

[1] Hatzfeld and Darmesteter, II, 2028; Godefroy, X, 660. II, 12, 476: "C'est ce que disoit Antisthenes, qu'il falloit faire provision ou de sens pour entendre, ou de licol pour se pendre."

[2] Robert Estienne, *Les Mots françois selon l'ordre des lettres, ainsi qu'il les faut escrire, tournez en latin* (Paris, 1572). Nicot, *Thresor de la langve françoise tant ancienne que Moderne* (Douceur, 1606). Reproduced from the 1621 edition by Picard et Cie, Paris, 1960: "Sens, Vient de *sensus* Latin par apocope, & a les deux mesmes significations, car nous disons, les cinq sens de nature, *Quinque sensus quibus naturâ praediti fumus* &, Il a perdu le sens, *Mente captus est.* Mais il ne retient pas la généralité dudit Latin, car nous disons sentiment, pour le tast & le toucher, comme, Il a perdu le sentiment .... Et en l'autre signification nous disons sens & entendement conjointement, *Mens.*"

sens is closely associated with *entendement* as a complementary term and that distinctions between the two words are not always possible nor even applicable at times. Montaigne, in "De mesnager sa volonté," deplores the evil habit that makes certain individuals align their convictions and their judgment with their desires. He finds that "leur sens et entandement est entièrement estouffé en leur passion. Leur discretion n'a plus d'autre chois que ce qui leur rit et qui conforte leur cause" (III, 10, 991). "Discretion" or the power of discernment is a substitute for judgment in this illustration. It cannot function properly because its parent, "sens et entandement," has been overpowered. Judgment is the demonstration of "sens et entandement." Moreover, *sens*, *entendement*, and *jugement* are not identical because *jugement* or "discretion" depends upon "sens et entandement," and more importantly because "sens et entandement" constitute not two particular faculties but one entity. In this example, Montaigne utilizes a composite term, if not a stock phrase.

The expression "sens et entendement" is capable of semantic variation and dichotomy. In his *Discours de la servitude volontaire*, La Boétie attacks the suppression of liberty, both physical and intellectual:

> Le grand Turc s'est bien avisé de cela, que les livres & la doctrine donnent, plus que toute autre chose, aus hommes le sens & l'entendement de se reconnoistre & d'haïr la tirannie.[1]

The construction "le sens & l'entendement de" indicates a quality, an ability, not a faculty. An appreciation of the logic and rules of usage which lie behind these terms is further complicated by Montaigne and by most writers of his time. The locution "le sens & l'entendement de," as it appears in the preceding quotation, can be divided into its component parts in order that each member may evoke the same meaning.

In "De la cruauté," Montaigne recalls an Italian nobleman's description of various peoples at war; he maintained that "les Allemans et les Souysses, plus grossiers et plus lourds, n'avoyent le sens de se raviser, à peine lors mesmes qu'ils estoyent accablez soubs les coups" (II, 11, 405–406). Conversely, in "De la praesumption," Montaigne admits to a high degree of ineptitude in several matters. He would starve in a well-stocked kitchen, and in a passage which appears only in the 1580 edition, he finds himself lacking in horsemanship: "[je] foy grand doubte, quand j'auroy un cheval et son équipage, que j'eusse

[1] La Boétie, *Œuvres complètes*, ed. Paul Bonnefon (Bordeaux, 1892), p. 30.

l'entendement de l'accommoder pour m'en servir" (II, 17, 636). Both examples contain the same meaning; they imply a lack of intelligence, a lack of sense and of aptitude, although it could be argued that *entendement* seems to emphasize the notion of know-how. At any rate, the lack of "le sens de se raviser" gives rise to a more damning condemnation than "l'entendement de l'accommoder." If a discernible difference exists, it is one of degree and not of kind. The interchangeability of *sens* and *entendement* in the preceding examples indicates that there is no demonstrable variation nor progression within the expression "sens et entendement" in those cases which refer to a faculty or faculties.

The term *sens* has countless applications for Montaigne, and they need not all necessarily represent a form of mental capacity or activity. In general, the word may signify frame of mind or mood,[1] anticipation and hope,[2] sense and significance,[3] sensibility and sensitivity,[4] individual abilities and mental capacity,[5] idea,[6] senses,[7] and meaning.[8] Yet, of all the terms which Montaigne uses in order to exemplify an activity of the mind, *sens* is the one which he employs the least; it appears only 60 times in the *Essais* whereas *entendement* is used 84 times.

The notion of *sens* (*sense*) seems to be the equal of *jugement*; indeed, Montaigne's manipulation of these terms in "De la praesumption," as our analysis will tend to demonstrate, leaves little room for equivocation. On the other hand, certain aspects of *sens* tend to relegate it to a more basic, less important role where it has connotations that are not

[1] II, 12, 549: "Les prescheurs sçavent que l'emotion qui leur vient en parlant, les anime vers la creance, et qu'en cholere nous nous adonnons plus à la deffence de nostre proposition, l'imprimons en nous et l'embrassons avec plus de vehemence et d'approbation que nous ne faisons estant en nostre sens froid et reposé."

[2] III, 2, 792: "Quand mes amis s'adressent à moy pour estre conseillez, je le fay librement et clairement, sans m'arrester, comme faict quasi tout le monde, à ce que, la chose estant hazardeuse, il peut advenir au rebours de mon sens, par où ils ayent à me faire reproche de mon conseil."

[3] I, 26, 145–146: "Il m'advint l'autre jour de tomber sur un tel passage. J'avois trainé languissant après des parolles Françoises si exangues, si descharnées et si vuides de matiere et de sens que ce n'estoient voirement que parolles Françoises."

[4] III, 10, 980: "J'espouse, et me passionne par consequant, de peu de choses. J'ay la veuë clere, mais je l'attache à peu d'objects; le sens delicat et mol."

[5] I, 56, 307: "L'un de noz historiens Grecs accuse justement son siecle de ce que les secrets de la religion Chrestienne estoient espandus enmy la place, és mains des moindres artisans; que chacun en peut debattre et dire selon son sens."

[6] III, 5, 840: "Pourquoy n'orront elles noz offres et noz demandes autant qu'elles se contienent sous le devoir de la modestie? Que va lon devinant qu'elles sonnent au dedans quelque sens plus libre?"

[7] I, 3, 23: "Heureux, qui sçachent resjouyr et gratifier leur sens par l'insensibilité, et vivre de leur mort."

[8] III, 13, 1096: "La gentille inscription dequoy les Atheniens honorerent la venue de Pompeius en leur ville, se conforme à mon sens."

principally related to *jugement*. However, *sens*, *jugement*, and *entendement* are identical and interchangeable in cases in which Montaigne chooses to delineate insanity, loss or alteration of senses, and distortion of reality.[1]

Montaigne usually refers to *sens*, *bon sens*, and *sens commun*; it is particularly the expression *sens commun* which gives *sens* a meaning not associated with *jugement*. In "Du pedantisme," Montaigne ridicules empty-headed pedagogues:

Mon vulgaire Perigordin appelle fort plaisamment "Lettreferits" ces sçavanteaux, comme si vous disiez "lettreferus," ausquels les lettres ont donné un coup de marteau, comme on dict. De vray, le plus souvent ils semblent estre ravalez, mesmes du sens commun (I, 25, 138).

Sens commun humanizes man. For La Boétie, *sens commun* is the distinctive trait of humanity, one to be equated with facial characteristics.[2] It is *sens commun* that distinguishes man from the underprivileged category of animal life as well as from the state of insensate madness.

However, *sens commun* is an untrained, native ability. It is an innate, instinctive, and intuitive demonstration of basic universal reason. It is in this sense that Montaigne uses it in "De la vanité":

Nos humeurs ne sont pas trop vaines, qui sont plaisantes; quelles qu'elles soient qui contentent constamment un homme capable de sens commun, je ne sçaurois avoir le coeur de le pleindre (III, 9, 976).

Most people, unless they are mentally deformed, are born with this ordinary degree of intelligence. It is not to be confused with sense or common sense, a quality which Montaigne usually attributes to the "homme d'entendement," but which he more customarily associates with the "peuple." The "vulgaire," the "peuple," have a practical sense born of experience, repetition, and assimilated examination. Although simple in its mechanics, it is not an instinctive ability. It avoids rigorous reasoning and logic and thrives in the patient, unemotional, and world-weary acceptance of life and of things as they are. Montaigne comes to admire and respect this "peuple" with its "bon sens."

Sens, like *jugement*, can be "natural." In the "Apologie de Raimond Sebond," Montaigne uses it with reference to the discursively linear reasoning of a fox about to test the strength of a frozen river:

[1] II, 12, 475: "Son frere Crito l'ayant faict remettre en son meilleur sens, il regrettoit cette sorte de condition en laquelle il avoit vescu plein de liesse et descharge de tout desplaisir."

[2] La Boétie, p. 49: "est il au monde rien moins supportable que cela, je ne dis pas à un homme de coeur, je ne dis pas à un bien né, mais seulement à un qui ait le sens commun, ou, sans plus, la face d'homme?"

n'aurions nous pas raison de juger ... que c'est une ratiocination et consequence tirée du sens naturel: Ce qui fait bruit, se remue; ce qui se remue, n'est pas gelé; ce qui n'est pas gelé, est liquide, et ce qui est liquide, plie soubs le faix (II, 12, 438)?

The progression of propositions within the fox's reasoning is the effect of "discours" or reflection, an attribute of "sens naturel." Again, as in the case of *jugement*, the adjective "naturel" indicates the basic capability to think, to reason. One imagines that perhaps *sens naturel* and *jugement naturel* are not readily identifiable. In the case of *sens*, the recipient is an animal; on the other hand, *jugement naturel* is used in the case of a child. What one may expect from both is a very different matter. *Sens naturel* is an unchanging capacity; like reason, it is a mechanism. *Jugement* rests upon a much broader base of consumed human activity. There is an inescapable aura of instinct and finiteness about *sens naturel* and *sens* in apposition with *jugement*

The most interesting and intriguing aspect of a relationship between *sens* and *jugement* is found in "De la praesumption." This essay reveals the vital point of the problem, for it contains a highly significant transposition of terms. Montaigne, with tongue in cheek, continues to emphasize and outline his "médiocrité":

ce seul par où je m'estime quelque chose, c'est ce en quoy jamais homme ne s'estima deffaillant: ma recommendation est vulgaire, commune et populaire, car qui a jamais cuidé avoir faute de *sens*? Ce seroit une proposition qui impliqueroit en soy de la contradiction.... Il ne fut jamais crocheteur ny femmelette qui ne pensast avoir assez de *sens* pour sa provision. Nous reconnoissons aysėement ės autres l'advantage du courage, de la force corporelle, de l'experience, de la disposition, de la beauté; mais l'advantage du *jugement*, nous ne le cedons à personne; et les raisons qui partent du simple *discours naturel* en autruy, il nous semble qu'il n'a tenu qu'à regarder de ce costé là, que nous les ayons trouvées.... les simples productions de l'*entendement*, chacun pense qu'il estoit en luy de les rencontrer toutes pareilles, et en apperçoit malaisement le poids et la difficulté (II, 17, 640).[1]

A few lines later, he further remarks: "on dit communément que le plus juste partage que nature nous aye fait de ses graces, c'est celuy du sens: car il n'est aucun qui ne se contente de ce qu'elle luy en a distribué" (II, 17, 641). In both passages, the term *sens* replaces the original *jugement* after 1588. The second occurrence of *sens* in the first passage remains throughout all successive editions, while the other psychological terms, that is *jugement*, *discours naturel*, and *entendement* encounter no alteration.

On the surface, these words seem correlative. Another occurrence of *entendement*, also omitted after 1588, reinforces this possibility: "Le

[1] Italics mine.

plus sot homme du monde pense autant avoir d'entendement que le plus habile" (II, 17, 640). It is difficult to imagine or find a more furbished passage, in terms of psychological words, in the *Essais*. Prior to the post-1588 corrections, the statement "les simples productions de l'entendement" read "les simples productions *du discours et* de l'entendement." The terms *sens* and *jugement* suggest homogeneity; the substitution of one term for the other, while the other terms remain constant, supports this. However, it is because the other words do not change that one questions the reason or the need for exchange in both instances. *Sens* must have a distinct meaning, at least within its specific context; these variants suggest a concern with the exact meaning of terms, even if we can't always grasp the content of that concern.

If Montaigne had also converted the second occurrence of *jugement* to *sens*, the reasoning would seem less obscure, as a few words in the second passage tend to indicate. In the first place, *nature* and *graces* destroy any notion of similarity between *sens* and the concept of judgment as presented in this study. For Montaigne, judgment is not imparted to man as part of his lot in life. Moreover, judgment has nothing whatever to do with "nature"; to say the least, one can scarcely conceive of it as a distributed good. Montaigne's irony, humorously directed at man's blind self-satisfaction, correctly alights upon the word *sens* because Montaigne thinks of it in terms of the mind, the intelligence, something to be valued, yet less than judgment. By means of irony, *sens*, which might otherwise be the equivalent of *jugement*, is shown to be inferior to *jugement*, for one of judgment's most trenchant and characteristic attributes is that of self-awareness.

Nevertheless, the second instance of *jugement* remains. Although Montaigne does not make a virtue of consistency, at least where his work is concerned, it seems that he has a very simple idea in mind. Judgment is not a self-sufficient, stationary, faculty or quality. The many who foolishly ("crocheteur," "femmelette") pride themselves in the possession of *sens* impose a limitation upon it and themselves ("assez de sens pour sa provision"). An awareness of self and of its limitations would compel *sens* to refrain from self-glorification and embellishment. Its inability to know and control itself can lead it to fatuity. Montaigne substitutes *sens* for *jugement* because self-awareness, their marked difference, does not permit judgment the self-deluding luxury of universal equality.

It may also be possible that the emergence of *sens* parallels Montaigne's diminishing castigation of the common people. He admires the "bon sens" which directs the "peuple" about him. Their unerring sense of practical philosophy replaces philosophical and abstract reasoning. Native intelligence can guide man.

In the practical application of what one learns at the hands of life, intellectually and morally, *sens* can and does equal *jugement. Sens* is a spontaneous manifestation of reason; it sees things as they are, unequivocally. Its strong sense of *mesure* makes it feel inherently the truth or falsehood of new phenomena:

La renommé ne se prostitue pas à si vil conte.... Le marbre eslevera vos titres tant qu'il vous plaira, pour avoir faict rapetasser un pan de mur ou descroter un ruisseau public, mais non pas les hommes qui ont du sens (III, 10, 1000–1001).

On the other hand, the existence, formation, and acquisition of *sens* is less demanding psychologically in that *sens* is unaware of, and does not contribute to, the process. *Sens* equals the accuracy and pertinency of judgment, but it lacks knowledge of itself. Although it can be the equivalent of judgment, it is more likely that Montaigne considers it an invaluable and acceptable substitute. Judgment is an active faculty which constantly questions itself and all of life; *sens* is an attribute, a guiding principle.

RAISON AND DISCOURS

While *sens* is customarily presented in a good light, *raison* and its affiliate *discours* are usually envisioned as the iniquitous intellectualities which paralyze judgment and lead man away from a true appreciation of his individual nature and humanness. The whole of the "Apologie de Raimond Sebond" is devoted to the examination, trial, and condemnation of reason; man has nefariously attempted to extend the boundaries of his limited capabilities, all in the name of reason. Yet Montaigne does not attack reason in its essence; properly controlled and guided, reason in and of itself can be a force for good. On the contrary, Montaigne unflaggingly pursues and defames the uses which are made of reason and the prerogatives and powers which man claims for it. Hence the intense prosecution of reason which unifies the "Apologie" thematically creates an ideational duality. The same reason which, when allowed to reign unchecked, entices man to denaturalize himself, is also capable of teaching him how to live according to his nature and of raising him beyond himself. Accordingly, *raison*, an indispensable aspect of judgment, is occasionally utilized to replace *jugement*; that is, they become ideational equivalents. On the other hand, *raison* can be the object of *jugement*'s primary correctional concern.

Ambivalence and sinuosity best characterize reason and Montaigne's concomitant treatment of its role and possibilities. Reason remains a contradiction in terms, for its agility is too easily identified with falsehood and evil and its seriousness and reflective ability are too quickly subsumed under judgment and regarded as "natural," true, and good. Montaigne tends to equate reason and nature on an existential level; however, reason, simultaneously a part and partner of judgment, must become a form of "second nature," if man is to profit from it. Something less than judgment, yet often its equal, it is asked to become what it already is or can be, that is *jugement*, and frequently *sens* and *entendement*, themselves idealized and recommended forms of "second nature." Reason is a living dialectic, a contradiction of opposites engulfed in a process of continual resolution.

Reason is both itself and *discours*, "raisonnable" and "raisonneuse." While reason evolves to the extent that Montaigne more frequently thinks of it as the means to man's terrestrial salvation rather than damnation, *discours* remains for him an entity to be carefully and closely watched. Although Montaigne does occasionally use *discours* in the positive sense of reason and reflection, he never ceases to suspect its individual activity and adherence to the standards established and maintained by judgment.

The etymology of *discours*, already noted in this study,[1] leads Montaigne to associate *discours* with the tenuous and disordered wanderings and abstractions of the mind. *Discours* frequently finds itself engaged in futile debate; judgment's role is to restrict its erratic and mindless behavior and mold it as a constructive and effective outlet for the demonstration of man's ability to reason systematically and cogently. In this manner, *discours* occasionally accompanies *jugement* and facilitates the articulation of its choice. The pejorative connotations of *discours* may be due in part to Montaigne's recollection that the Latin etymon of *raison* is *ratiō*, that is calculation and computation.[2]

Montaigne generally equates *raison* and *discours*.[3] On occasion, he

[1] Chapter II, p. 49.

[2] Bloch and von Wartburg, p. 524.

[3] I, 23, 109: "J'estime qu'il ne tombe en l'imagination humaine aucune fantasie si forcenée qui ne rencontre l'exemple de quelque usage public, et par consequent que nostre discours n'estaie et ne fonde." Montaigne substitutes *discours* for *raison* after 1588.

uses both terms concurrently and any semblance of a distinction is difficult to establish.[1] At times, *raison* is seen to contain *discours*. In "De l'art de conferer," Montaigne reiterates his belief in the causality of hazard in the conduct of human affairs and in the formation and control of one's desires and actions: "Ma volonté et mon discours se remue tantost d'un air, tantost d'un autre, et y a plusieurs de ces mouvemens qui se gouvernent sans moy. Ma raison a des impulsions et agitations journallieres et casuelles" (III, 8, 912–913). It is probable that *raison* equals *jugement*, for Montaigne notes that his judgment is moved by disturbances over which he can exercise no control. Moreover, the context indicates that *raison* is a distinctive and personal intellectual and psychological entity; *discours* is but a part of the whole.

Montaigne's conglomeration of psychological terms occasionally seems to indicate a distinction or rather progression between the various words. In the "Apologie," Montaigne remarks that man deludes himself into thinking that his intelligence makes him superior to the animals: "Ce n'est donc plus par la raison, par le discours et par l'ame que nous excellons sur les bestes; c'est par nostre beauté, nostre beau teint et nostre belle disposition de membres" (II, 12, 465). *Discours* is not *raison* nor is it a part or an extension of *raison*. It is a separate and autonomous body. Perhaps *discours* implies the capability of rational inference as opposed to *raison*'s ability to reason; this slight distinction tends to indicate the forward thrust or resolving motion of *discours* in contrast with the steadfast and abstract argumentative ability of *raison*. Moreover, Montaigne seems to establish a hierarchy of values or importance within this specific progression of terms so that one is inclined to consider *raison* less significant than *discours* and *ame*. No doubt, Montaigne values *ame* above *discours* and *raison*. It has already been noted that Montaigne finds it difficult to distinguish between *ame* and the most important of man's faculties, that is *jugement*. If *discours* surpasses *raison* in significance, it may be that Montaigne tends to equate *discours* with *jugement*; the mobile, concrete aspects of *discours* make of it a more apt substitute for *jugement* than *raison*. Certainly, *ame* is juxtaposed with *discours* and *raison*; perhaps the amalgamation of the two discursive terms constitutes *jugement*.

When the terms *raison*, *jugement*, and *ame* are used in conjunction with one another, they appear to be interchangeable throughout the *Essais*. Although Montaigne approaches the possibilities of reason

[1] II, 12, 424–425: "Or, nos raisons et nos discours humains, c'est comme la matiere lourde et sterile: la grace de Dieu en est la forme; c'est elle qui y donne la façon et le pris."

negatively in the "Apologie," he also describes it as a less than inconsequential and ephemeral quantity. Reason has an abode and occupies an important part of man's psyche: "Elle est en l'ame, et partie ou effect d'icelle: car la vraye raison est essentielle" (II, 12, 523). Soul is the divine aspect which links man to God; in this example,[1] reason is an apersonal principle demonstrated and controlled by God and instilled in man by the grace of God. Montaigne discusses reason on many discrete levels. The adjectives "vraye" and "essentielle" attest a form of universal reason, an underlying and pre-established causality within man's world. Man's personal reason, his own existential faculty, is the product and demonstration of an essential and universal reason imparted to all men. Reason, or the ability to reason, as opposed to *jugement,* is an essential part of man; its close association with the soul makes it attend to all of man's functions. Reason contributes to man's intellectual and moral sustenance; it is man's nature, his essence and existence. Judgment becomes the emergence and self-assertion of man's reason. In this sense, reason and judgment, in their association with the soul, are identical and inseparable. However, *raison* precedes *jugement.* While *raison* and perhaps *soul* are mastered, *jugement* is formed.The difference is fundamental.

Another relationship between judgment and reason depends upon the persuasive powers of *discours.* In "Coustume de l'isle de Cea," Montaigne relates several anecdotes which demonstrate the effectiveness of an intangible but catalytic agent which frequently causes disparate wills to unite in public gatherings and act as one body: "Ce que le discours ne feroit en chacun, il le faict en tous; l'ardeur de la société ravissant les particuliers jugements" (II, 3, 341). It is the role of *discours* to persuade *jugement* of the applicability of a choice or action. Indeed, it is because persuasion becomes an end in itself rather than the means to an end that judgment normally reacts ponderously and in a leisurely and detached fashion. *Jugement* is activated, awakened by *discours. Jugement* reacts to the efforts of *discours.* In the preceding passage, a supernumerary entity, that is psychological and emotional frenzy, disengages the proper actuating capacity of *discours* while simultaneously nullifying individual judgment. Neither functions without the other. Certainly, *discours* often borders upon the world of

[1] Another example appears in this phrase from III, 12, 1037: "la semence de la raison universelle empreinte en tout homme non desnaturé."

fantasy and imagination, inaudibly mesmerizing judgment; [1] however, in this example from "Coustume de l'isle de Cea," *discours* is as affected as its customary possessor.

Discours, like *raison*, explores and establishes all the possibilities and the pertinency of new appearances and ideas. Montaigne suggests that it is frequently in this capacity that it impedes the orderly progression of judgment's analysis: "Il ne faut pas laisser au jugement de chacun la cognoissance de son devoir; il le lui faut prescrire, non pas le laisser choisir à son discours" (II, 12, 467). *Discours* and *jugement* appear to be synonymous only superficially. The notion of choice in the case of *discours* does not incorporate the process of decision. Decision, that is the establishment of what is to be accepted, remains the distinctive trait and prerogative of judgment. "Cognoissance" is the product of judgment; *discours* prepares the possibility of ultimate and final choice which is judgment's alone. *Discours* is visualized as the exteriorization of the inner intellectual journey which reason effects within the mind. However, when *raison* and *discours* appear conjunctively, one is induced to categorize *raison* as an impersonal entity, a principle of universal reasonableness, and *discours* as its manifestation within the individual. In this way, Montaigne is able to incorporate "reasonableness," an axiom, and "reason," an individual occurrence; semantically, the possibility is significant since Montaigne concurrently maintains a duality of consequential application within the outline of personal reason. Consequently, the relation of judgment to reason in any given circumstance rests upon the perception of the notional and semantic levels of *raison*.

Montaigne's scathing rebuke of reason in the "Apologie de Raimond Sebond" persists throughout the *Essais*; it is not limited to a specific area or period within the development of his thought. Montaigne recognizes that reason is an intellectual possibility, a tool which must be mastered and guided: "la raison fournit d'apparence à divers effects. C'est un pot à deux ances, qu'on peut saisir à gauche et à dextre" (II, 12, 565–566). Montaigne's vocabulary emphasizes reason as a means which enables another faculty, namely *jugement*, to operate effectively; the verb *saisir* indicates the availability of reason, and, more importantly, the need to supervise it well, for the fatuous, insensate, and nefarious performance of reason is attributable to a poorly formed

[1] III, 11, 1004: "Nostre discours est capable d'estoffer cent autres mondes et d'en trouver les principes et la contexture. Il ne luy faut ny matiere, ny base; laissez le courre: il bastit aussi bien sur le vuide que sur le plain, et de l'inanité que de matiere."

judgment. In "De la praesumption," Montaigne observes that even Socrates is capable of misinterpreting and negating truth: "La raison humaine est un glaive double et dangereux. Et en la main mesme de Socrate, son plus intime et plus familier amy, voyez à quand de bouts c'est un baston" (II, 17, 638).

The image of the sword contains all the pratices which Montaigne imputes to reason. It is a weapon, an implement of human thought which can betray the one who wields it; in and of itself, it is a useful, necessary, but hazardous corollary to man's *sens* and *entendement*. Left to its own devices, it reasons, as it must, the logical soundness of all positions. Reason is a "glaive," an instrument, an extension of one's *entendement* which, of necessity and by its nature, must be encircled and manipulated. As Montaigne clearly recognizes in "De la coustume et de ne changer aisément une loy receuë," "la raison humaine est une teinture infuse environ de pareil pois à toutes nos opinions et moeurs, de quelque forme qu'elles soient: infinie en matiere, infinie en diversité" (I, 23, 110). The appropriate relativity of reason remains to be extricated and interpreted at the hands of judgment:

> J'appelle tousjours raison cette apparence de discours que chacun forge en soy; cette raison, de la condition de laquelle il y en peut avoir cent contraires autour d'un mesme subject, c'est un instrument de plomb et de cire, alongeable, ployable et accommodable à tous biais et à toutes mesures; il ne reste que la suffisance de le sçavoir contourner (II, 12, 548).

The indispensable "suffisance" for the proper allocation and utilization of reason is judgment. Reason explores and pursues the cause of things; judgment seeks truth.

Montaigne attacks the reason which glories in its sheltered and vain capacity to rationalize abstractions. Montaigne cannot abide the reason which does not bear the heavy stamp of the individual, that is that reason whose sole purpose is not the guidance of man. It is to the inanity of reason that Montaigne opposes judgment. When reason is firmly implanted within the individual and incorporates the sum and substance of his intellectual and moral being, it acts responsibly in order to guide man; it becomes the equivalent of *jugement*:

> La philosophie ne pense pas avoir mal employé ses moyens quand elle a rendu à la raison la souveraine maistrise de nostre ame et l'authorité de tenir en bride nos appetits (II, 33, 705).

In "De l'institution des enfans," Montaigne declares that the true function of philosophy is the training of judgment. It is specifically within the realm of human conduct, both intellectual and moral, that *raison* and *jugement* become absolutely and perfectly synonymous:

Je fay coustumierement entier ce que je fay et marche tout d'une piece; je n'ay guere de mouvement qui se cache et desrobe à ma raison, et qui ne se conduise à peu près par le consentement de toutes mes parties (III, 2, 790).

la seule raison doit avoir la conduite de nos inclinations. J'ay, de ma part, le goust estrangement mousse à ces propensions qui sont produites en nous sans l'ordonnance et entremise de nostre jugement (II, 8, 366).

esclave, je ne le doibts estre que de la raison, encore ne puis-je bien en venir à bout (III, 1, 772).

Nevertheless, one cannot help but notice differences in the usage of *raison* in the previous lines. In the first passage, perhaps because of the strong sense of individuality conveyed by the possessive adjective, *raison* is a personal faculty which supervises and unites the whole of man; not unlike *jugement*, it is centered within man, an inseparable part of his personality. On the other hand, the use of *raison* in the two succeeding quotations impresses one with the notion of truth and falsehood, good and evil, according to which the individual conducts himself; it is an abstract conviction, a rule of conduct, indeed a virtue, which presides over man's behavior. It inspires man to act according to its immutable tenets. However, it is the function of another entity, represented by *je* in the third passage, to engage and exercise it. Needless to say, although Montaigne occasionally uses *jugement* in an identical fashion, one is often left with the impression that *jugement*, both the faculty and the quality, is somewhat more unitary than *raison*, divided as it is by its varied applications.

Invariably, Montaigne's reader confronts relationships whose motives remain impenetrable. Moreover, the connections are not limited to *raison* and *jugement*, for they also include *sens* and *entendement*. The frequent synonymity of so many terms tends to complicate irrevocably particular affiliations. In the "Apologie de Raimond Sebond," Montaigne proves the inanity of man's argumentative powers by assembling numerous examples of inconsequential syllogisms: "Jugeons par là ce que nous avons à estimer de l'homme, de son sens et de sa raison" (II, 12, 527). It is difficult to establish a meaningful distinction between *sens* and *raison*; they appear to be identical faculties. One might conceive of *sens* as *entendement* or intelligence, for intellect is not reason. However, in "De l'art de conferer," *entendement*, in the sense of *jugement*, is equated with *raison*: "Ce que j'adore moymesmes aus Roys, c'est la foule de leurs adorateurs. Toute inclination et soubmission leur est deuë, sauf celle de l'entendement. Ma raison n'est pas duite à se courber et flechir, ce sont mes genoux" (III, 8, 913). Because this example contains separate sentences, one can attribute the change to a desire for lexical variation. In "De la vanité," Montaigne discusses the rewards of unfettered and free choice. He declares that his sovereign will doubly profit from his service if he, Montaigne, believes of his own free will that such is his duty or desire: "J'en sers plus gayement mon prince par ce que c'est par libre eslection de mon jugement et de ma raison" (III, 9, 966). If *jugement* and *raison* are as identical as they seem to be, one can only conclude that *raison* is a perfunctory appendage which Montaigne frequently adds to other terms which suggest an activity of the mind.

In general, Montaigne holds that reason, like *sens*, can be the natural instinct of humanity, the force or quality which can lead man to happiness. To say the least, Montaigne's mounting confidence in the innate abilities and native intelligence of man leads him to believe in a fairly equal representation of reason in all human beings. All men can discover truth, for "la semence de la raison universelle empreinte en tout homme non desnaturé" (III, 12, 1037) [1] insures them of a universal, reasonable, and static order. Reason is both within man and outside of him; it is internal and external, particular and universal. Judgment, an entity which is formed and which remains perpetually adjustable, is the faculty which effects a reconciliation between the two. Otherwise, individual reason and universal or natural reason could very well find themselves inexorably opposed to one another. Certainly, Montaigne does not conceive of universal reason as *jugement*; at most, he infrequently equates the judicious employment of personal reason with *jugement.*

In summary, *discours* and *raison* frequently imply uncontrolled and abstract thinking, authoritarian but questionable logic, a lack of human "reasonableness"; a blind penchant for presumptuous, ambiguous, and poor reasoning is the usual connotation of *raison* in the "Apologie." Conversely, *raison* also infers sound reflection and reasonableness; in this sense, *raison* incorporates all the attributes of *jugement.* However, reason *per se* is an essential unit of judgment; it is the intellectual and often moral means by which man *can* be guided. Basically, *jugement* is a trained, experienced, matured, self-disciplined, "humanized" *raison.*

[1] See p. 128 for a discussion of Montaigne's use of universal reason.

CONSCIENCE

For Montaigne, man's intellectual life would be of little value if its primary purpose, its goal, and its only worthwhile achievement were not the development of conscience, the establishment of man's moral life. In "De l'institution des enfans" and, indeed, throughout the *Essais* there circulates the desire, the aspiration to instill in man a strong scrupulous sense of personal probity. It is for this reason that Montaigne conceives of judgment not only as an intellectual faculty but also as a moral power capable of distinguishing between good and evil. Hence, *conscience*, the faculty which awakens and guides man's perception of what is morally right and wrong, not only for the individual but also in an absolute sense, is both an independent entity and a function of *jugement*. Because the role of *conscience* is an innate function of *jugement*, one wonders if Montaigne attributes a distinct or different meaning to *conscience* when he employs it independently; this problem of terminology appears particularly in Book III in which Montaigne's use of the term *conscience* doubles that of Books I and II combined. A somewhat more perplexing development is that in which *jugement* and *conscience* emerge concurrently and yet appear to play separate parts.

Conscience includes three distinct levels of moral activity within the individual. Perhaps the first is no more than emotional or psychological, for it manifests itself outwardly and becomes an observable part of man's behavior. In "De la conscience," Montaigne recalls having encountered, during France's civil wars, a nobleman of the Protestant party who pretended to be of the Catholic party. As Montaigne emphasizes, there was nothing about this man that might make one place him in one camp or the other. It was his conscience that betrayed him:

> cettuy-cy en avoit une frayeur si esperduë, et je le voiois si mort à chasque rencontre d'hommes à cheval et passage de villes qui tenoient pour le Roy, que je devinay en fin que c'estoient alarmes que sa conscience luy donnoit. Il sembloit à ce pauvre homme qu'au travers de son masque et des croix de sa cazaque on iroit lire jusques dans son coeur ses secrettes intentions. Tant est merveilleux l'effort de la conscience! Elle nous faict trahir, accuser et combattre nous mesme, et, à faute de tesmoing estrangier, elle nous produit, contre nous (II, 5, 346).

Conscience here is the knowledge, an interior perception and emotion, that one is engaged in a perilous activity. It is doubtful that the nobleman is concerned with the good or evil of his impersonation; the "alarmes" of his conscience are born of fear and lack of self-control.

To be sure, he recognizes that his behavior is reprehensible and not without reproach; however, he cowers before men's eyes out of a misguided sense of self-preservation. Inner turmoil and the lack of emotional tranquillity, not a sense of what is right and what is wrong, reveal this man's true identity. Conscience is one's awareness of one's personal, true, and innermost thoughts, the self-illuminating recognition of one's knowledge of oneself as opposed to that of the world which surrounds one. Indeed, the anecdotes which Montaigne presents in "De la conscience" disclose immense amounts of self-assurance rather than the morally beneficial activity of conscience.

The second activity of *conscience* affords man no more control over it than the first. This is the religious application of *conscience*, perhaps best characterized by remorse, that is the knowledge or feeling that one has transgressed divine laws. Man conceives and formulates these religious and holy precepts, and he identifies *conscience* with the seat of inevitable moral anguish and fear of divine reprisal which accompanies offenses or sin. Speaking specifically of sin ("péché") and not of crime or offense, Montaigne remarks that "à mesme qu'on prend le plaisir au vice, il s'engendre un desplaisir contraire en la conscience, qui nous tourmente de plusieurs imaginations penibles, veillans et dormans" (II, 5, 347). This aspect of *conscience* is given minimal exposure in the *Essais*. When in doubt, Montaigne prefers a "natural" conscience, one which man develops and endows himself, to a rigidly "religious" acceptation of conscience. *Conscience* or one's moral and religious status in the eyes of God is seen to best advantage in Montaigne's remembrance of La Boétie's death. La Boétie wishes to commend his soul to God in the presence of a priest:

> Ayant mis ordre à mes biens, encores me faut il penser à ma conscience. Je suis Chrestien, je suis Catholique: tel ay vescu, tel suis-je deliberé de clorre ma vie. Qu'on me face venir un prestre, car je ne veux faillir à ce dernier devoir d'un Chrestien.[1]

The conception of *conscience* which particularly concerns Montaigne is that which may be called natural or moral as opposed to religious notions of conscience. Montaigne maintains that concepts of good and evil are relative; they are not the product of innate ideas: "Les loix de la conscience, que nous disons naistre de nature, naissent de la coustume" (I, 23, 114). Usually, Montaigne's references to *conscience* imply man's individual conscience, his personal notions of right and wrong

[1] "Fragment d'une lettre," *Œuvres complètes*, ed. Albert Thibaudet and Maurice Rat (Paris, 1962), pp. 1352–1353.

which have been acquired by means of reason and experience. For Montaigne, there is no absolute morality; the dictates of conscience are consequently relative.

One may conceive of Montaigne's morality as a secular one. Devoid of religious connotations, man's conscience is the faculty or function of judgment which establishes his sense and knowledge of proper conduct and moral rectitude. Montaigne's *conscience* is none other than *raison*, in the good sense of the term, applied to questions of morality, a morality which is evolved by means of reason. Man's moral sense, his natural conscience, creates precepts and ordinances which are as binding upon the individual as if they were immutable heavenly proscriptions. Indeed, conscience is man's individual tribunal, the faculty which guides the progression of his integrity and goodness as reason and his nature conceive them.

Conscience is man's sense of having done what was necessary, what had to be done, in any given situation. Conscience is a testimonial of goodness, of virtue. It procreates a feeling of well-being within the individual:

> Il y a certes je ne sçay quelle congratulation de bien faire qui nous resjouit en nous mesmes et une fierté genereuse qui accompaigne la bonne conscience.... Ces tesmoignages de la conscience plaisent; et nous est grand benefice que cette esjouyssance naturelle, et le seul payement qui jamais ne nous manque (III, 2, 784–785).

Montaigne applies the term *conscience* to that body of knowledge which serves to fashion man into a virtuous being. *Conscience* is the most impenetrable part of man, that which is his alone to know and enjoy. It is *conscience* which savors the tranquillity of a mind and soul at peace with one another. Conversely, it is also *conscience* which reels under the impact of moral disturbance and decrepitude within the individual.

The role of conscience is to guide man's moral development. When new phenomena appear before judgment, conscience attempts to extricate the moral and spiritual truth which they involve. It deliberates as to how it can best improve man; the decision which it registers becomes an indelible part of man's spirit. Hence, *conscience* is both a moral arbitrator and, perhaps more significantly, an activator, for it induces man to act silently and decisively in behalf of his spiritual gratification: "c'est le contentement qu'une conscience bien reglée reçoit en soy de bien faire" (II, 16, 607).

Because *conscience* is the preservor of man's integrity, it is not to be tampered with lightly. The "prostitution de conscience," as Montaigne calls it, can endanger all of man's moral existence. Any infraction of the rules of conscience threatens to corrupt the whole man. Transgressions of moment and time lead to violations by "complexion." Conscience is so prized that "toute personne d'honneur choisit de perdre plustost son honneur, que de perdre sa conscience" (II, 16, 614). Occasionally, the injunctions of conscience must be set aside for reasons of state. Deplorable as they are, they frequently impose themselves upon the most scrupulous men. Man's individual sense of what is morally good and evil in a specific occurrence can be momentarily suspended in the interests of a collective body; however, man does so at his own risk, and he is never permitted to do so solely in his personal behalf:

> Ce sont dangereux exemples, rares et maladifves exceptions à nos reigles naturelles. Il y faut ceder, mais avec grande moderation et circonspection; aucune utilité privée n'est digne pour laquelle nous facions cet effort à nostre conscience; la publique, bien lors qu'elle est et très-apparente et très-importante (III, 1, 778).

The dignity of the individual is constantly the uppermost concern of Montaigne's mind. Nothing must be allowed to reduce it, to obscure it, to stifle it. Conscience, that is the "bonne conscience," is the provider and guardian of human dignity and goodness. Man is free only in the sense that he presides over his own destiny.

Montaigne recognizes that the improvement of man is a trying task because the individual is quick to supplant the pertinency of conscience by subtler, lighter, and less difficult accessions to experience:

> Sentez lire un discours de philosophie; l'invention, l'eloquence, la pertinence frape incontinent vostre esprit et vous esmeut; il n'y a rien qui chatouille ou poigne vostre conscience; ce n'est pas à elle qu'on parle, est-il pas vray? Si disoit Ariston que ny une esteuve, ny une leçon n'est d'aucun fruict si elle ne nettoye et ne descrasse (III, 9, 967–968).

The profound moral and spiritual change which reason and experience must exercise within the individual is the domain of conscience. *Conscience* is not a secret and uncontrollable testimony which the soul renders of itself. It is an active and operative faculty; it not only witnesses and registers but it also moves the moral fibers which permeate man. Man is induced to act according to his conscience and by his judgment.

Conscience is a function of judgment; it can also be a separate and autonomous faculty. Not all questions which properly belong to judgment's field of experience require the participation of conscience. By the same token, concepts formulated by *conscience* are not necessarily susceptible to the investigative powers and prerogatives of judgment. What man finds to be reasonable in conscience may escape the categories of truth and falsehood because the relativity of certain morally acceptable principles is a matter of reasonable acceptance rather than reasoned legislation. Montaigne refuses to judge the relative merits of the Ptolemaic and Copernican astronomical systems because neither is particularly significant to Montaigne's search for truth, not to mention his avowed incompetence in the matter; unquestionably, the concept of good and evil is not in contention. It is Montaigne's *conscience,* in and of itself, which makes of him a religious and political conservative; it is his *jugement* which establishes the conscientious relativity, both moral and intellectual, of his position. Sound conscience need not acquiesce to judgment; Descartes's "morale provisoire," a singular copy of Montaigne's conservatism and relativism, demonstrates this principle.

Conscience, like *jugement,* is frequently a quality rather than a function or a faculty. In "De l'institution des enfans," Montaigne characterizes conscience as the free and spontaneous recognition and admission that one is in error. It is likely that he tends to equate it with virtue and goodness: "Que sa conscience et sa vertu reluisent en son parler, et n'ayent que la raison pour guide" (I, 26, 154). The admonition to obey reason is a post-1588 addition. *Conscience* is goodness; it must be developed within the individual at the same time that his *jugement* is being formed and tested. It is not a part of him nor is it immediately accessible through general education. The inclusion of reason indicates that conscience is apt to stray and formulate moral laws that are beyond man's reach. It also stresses the natural, rational base of conscience. Conscience is not wisdom; hence, reasonableness must accompany the evolution of conscience. *Conscience* is not a law unto itself; its efforts must be sanctioned by reason. One's concept of good and evil is steeped in one's ability to recognize that which is reasonable, a principle which is far less durable but more flexible than that of *jugement.* It is small wonder that Montaigne entrusts the care of conscience to judgment.

Montaigne believes in the ability of conscience to judge correctly in the moral realm because reason is its guide, if not its guarantor. Since, in a sense, *conscience* is a synonym of *raison,* one wonders why he so frequently considers it necessary to use them conjunctively, as though one were asked to attach separate meanings to each. In "Du repentir," Montaigne distinguishes between momentary, spontaneous forms of sin and those which, through long repetition, have become an integral part of one's personality. The individual who is beset by "professional" sin does not truly seek repentance, for his repeated errors must require the acquiescence and collaboration of his entire being: "je ne puis pas concevoir qu'ils soient plantez si long temps en mesme courage sans que la raison et la conscience de celuy qui les possede, le veuille constamment et l'entende ainsi" (III, 2, 790). Either *raison* or *conscience* would seem to be sufficient; indeed, *jugement*, as it is conceptualized by Montaigne, seems more appropriate. Montaigne recognizes that morality is intellectually formulated and that one cannot err in conscience without the concomitant approval of reason. Montaigne's example stresses the fact that organic sin is willed; hence, it may be that *raison* functions as a substitute for will.

Throughout this study, it has been held that *jugement* individualizes and identifies man. *Conscience*, at least in part, fulfills the same function. In "Des plus excellens hommes," Montaigne firmly insists upon the high excellence of spirit which was attained by Epaminondas:

quant à ses meurs et conscience, il a de bien loing surpassé tous ceux qui se sont jamais meslé de manier affaires. Car en cette partie, qui seule doit estre principalement considérée, qui seule marque veritablement quels nous sommes, et laquelle je contrepoise seule à toutes les autres ensemble, il ne cede à aucun philosophe, non pas à Socrates mesme (II, 36, 735).

Conscience seems to equal *jugement* because it envelops one's true being ("quels nous sommes"). However, "en cette partie" refers to both "meurs et conscience," and undoubtedly Montaigne would consider that only their combination can equal the private and public self, that is *jugement*. *Meurs* unites with *entendement*, *sens*, and *conscience*, and it is only in this association that all four terms attain the possibility of replacing *jugement*; as single units, these terms remain too closely connected with their original meaning. At best, they are doubtful substitutes which do not carry the full and duplicate import of *jugement*.

Montaigne demands that order and clarity preside over the presentation of one's thoughts. Lack of order leads him to attach little importance to matter and meaning and a great deal of imperious and malicious attention to detail and form: "Il est impossible de traitter de bonne foy avec un sot. Mon jugement ne se corrompt pas seulement à la main d'un maistre si impetueux, mais aussi ma conscience" (III, 8, 903–904). Montaigne makes a definite distinction between *jugement* and *conscience*. When *jugement* fails to make itself understood and accepted intellectually, it knows better than to pursue its course. The better part of intellectual valor is disengagement and silence. Dismissal of *jugement*'s experience and better instinct embroils Montaigne's conscience so that he is no longer capable of judging intellectually; it also leads him to implicate and demean the whole of his moral sense. While both *jugement* and *conscience* include the ability to do good and evil, *conscience* seems to have an added defensive role. *Conscience* acts as an individual part of the psyche which is betrayed when judgment's first line of moral defense collapses. Until after 1588, the term *entendement* in "Du pedantisme" seemed to be sufficient to carry the full impact of Montaigne's meaning: "Nous ne travaillons qu'à remplir la memoire, et laissons l'entendement (C) et la conscience (A) vuide" (I, 25, 135). Because *entendement* appears to be the equivalent of *jugement*, it should include the activity of *conscience* in moral matters. Judgment and conscience are inseparable and cooperate indefatigably; usually, they constitute but one faculty. The addition of *conscience* may involve no more than Montaigne's desire to emphasize and extend the significance of what he does not consider memory to be. Certainly, the fact that Montaigne adds *conscience* to *entendement* indicates that *entendement* does not equal *jugement* in this specific context or that Montaigne attaches to *conscience* a moral meaning which he does not accredit to *entendement* and *jugement*.

In general, *conscience* refers to man's moral nature, a set of rules and ethics which man formulates himself and which should fall within the limits of his human nature. *Conscience* constitutes a practical code of conduct, one which man is capable of attaining and maintaining. Reason, nature, and conscience join together in order to permit man to attain the summit of which he is personally and inherently capable. Conscience strives to analyze the moral content and portent of new phenomena for the individual; it attempts to change the individual in order to make of him a better human being. Hence, *conscience*, like *jugement*, is an objective, a virtue or faculty which does not exist in and of itself but whose creation and perfection Montaigne consistently explains and requests. *Jugement* is both an intellectual and moral guide, analyzing and establishing the truth or falsehood, good and evil of new appearances; *conscience* concerns itself only with the morality of events and of man's actions.

Montaigne sketches the essential structural aspects of these particular psychological terms, but he does not elaborate their intrinsic associations nor does he relate their extraneous connections systematically and consciously. The relationships which pervade the *Essais* are imprecise and amorphous; the general idea which they afford is the result of associative similarities which link these terms according to form and meaning.

The principal psychological unit which concerns Montaigne is the faculty of judgment. The other terms constitute various capacities, often identical, which mediate among one another; they represent judgment in part or in whole as the context indicates. Judgment is not a simple, unitary faculty. It is a hierarchy of successively acquired and assimilated capabilities and qualities. Judgment is the intellectual and moral faculty which incorporates all of the individual's other psychological possibilities and characteristics. It is for this reason that the faculty of judgment is simultaneously the observer of self and the object of Montaigne's study. In the last analysis, it is the intellectual, moral, and psychological role of self-discovery and self-knowledge which distinguishes the concept of judgment from its ideational and semantic affiliates.

CONCLUSION

Analysis of the concept of judgment in the *Essais* emphasizes the complexity and richness of Montaigne's thought with regard to all activities of the mind. More significantly, a comparison of the principal psychological terms which describe and embody the intellectual, moral, and emotional characteristics of the psyche indicates that Montaigne does not merely use these words for the purpose of lexical variation. *Entendement, sens, raison,* and *jugement* can be synonymous within specific contexts; however, an examination of their general usage demonstrates that they are markedly different.

Entendement is the basic word for the description of mental activity; it includes all the discursive qualities of the mind. Generally, *entendement* refers to intelligence or intellect and particularly the sound demonstration of intelligence. Its primary function is that of conception rather than criticism. Montaigne usually regards *entendement* favorably. As a quality rather than a specific faculty, *entendement* is an epithet which implies sound and admirable thinking; it frequently describes a man both intellectually and socially.

Sens has numerous applications which do not represent a form of mental capacity. Within the semantic and ideational field of intellectual activity, it is closer to *jugement* than the other terms; in the realm of practical knowledge, *sens* can and does equal *jugement.* As a common denominator, *sens* represents the spontaneous manifestation of reason. It often implies untrained, native ability. *Sens* is also an innate, instinctive, and intuitive demonstration of sound reasoning. It is practical sense born of experience. Although *sens* is acquired, it does not contribute actively and consciously to its own creation. Montaigne considers *sens* to be the closest acceptable substitute for judgment.

Raison is usually used pejoratively; however, Montaigne generally attacks the uses which are made of reason and not reason in and of itself. *Raison* can connote sound reasoning and reasonableness as well as vain, ineffectual, and bad reasoning. Montaigne consistently berates the reason which revels in its futile ability to rationalize abstractions; he opposes judgment to the inanity of reason.

Conscience is both an independent faculty and a function of judgment. It generally denotes man's natural, individual, and personal notion of good and evil. *Conscience* is reason applied to questions of morality, a morality which of necessity is neither psychological nor religious but secular and relative. As a quality, it connotes personal goodness and virtue.

Jugement is the central and most important psychological term and concept in the *Essais*. It can indicate an act, a faculty, a quality, and frequently the seat of all intellectual, moral, and psychological life. The ability to distinguish truth and falsehood is its most general meaning both in the *Essais* and in the sixteenth century. However, for Montaigne, the meaning of *jugement* extends beyond the limits of a semantic framework; indeed, judgment is a concept and a theme which pervades the whole of the *Essais*.

Discussion with La Boétie and readings of Sebond, Seneca, Plutarch, and Cicero influence Montaigne's conceptualization of judgment in a general way. Sebond stresses the need of personal reflection and self-knowledge. While Seneca ridicules the inconstancy of judgment, he also emphasizes, as does Cicero, the security of self-reliance which judgment can provide. Plutarch demonstrates the application of judgment to the moral analysis of man.

In great part, Montaigne's skeptical nature, communicative penchant, desire to seek truth and innate ability to grasp it intuitively and deductively determine many of the attributes and operation of judgment. His antithetical way of thinking constantly opposes judgment and memory or "science." In this way, judgment is visualized as an intellectual "disponibilité," a form of ignorance which breeds inquisitiveness and objective dialogue. Judgment seeks knowledge, a beneficial "science," but the formation of judgment is by far the more important of the two. Knowledge, "science," memory are frequently sterile and futile abstract appendages, whereas judgment is material experience.

The essays "Du pedantisme" and "De l'institution des enfans" describe the means by which judgment, man's critical capacity, can be formed. Extensive exposure to all phenomena, constant observation and active participation, assiduous analysis and ponderous reflection, personal choice, and immediate and accurate comparison of new appearances with past experience lead to truth and reason, which are the manifestation and goal of judgment. Judgment is a progressive form of reason which changes as it experiences everything that can be affected by human action.

Judgment is closely associated with conscience. It must be able to determine good and evil, truth and falsehood, in men and in their actions; to judge is to seek intellectual, psychological, and moral knowledge. Judgment attempts to control and direct man's more prolific and less manageable faculties; hence, it enables man to rise above his condition. It is superior to the other faculties because it is able to recognize its strengths and weaknesses; knowledge of God and scrutiny of religious and political institutions are beyond its capability. Although it attempts to control all things human, it occasionally surrenders to superior instinct and mental exaltation; it frequently collapses before passion.

Because the development of judgment and the study of human nature are inseparable, judgment and self-study become interdependent. Because judgment's principal function evolves from inspection to introspection, self-study constitutes a major expansion of the role of judgment. Man's intellectual, psychological, and moral identity escapes disintegration within the timeless and spaceless analysis of judgment. The faculty of judgment enables man to discover the "natural" truth of his being; in the process, the two distinct, yet inseparable parts of personality, the "je" and the "moi," are reconciled. The viable fusion of judgment and self-knowledge creates man's moral and intellectual independence; inner harmony is the goal of judgment and the product of self-knowledge.

The notion of "essai," "essayer," that is to experience, depicts the role and primary activity of judgment, for the whole of life is the proper test of judgment. Judgment must orient man throughout the motion, change, and diversity of life. Ultimately, man's knowledge and moral worth is reflected in his ability to judge himself. It is for this reason that Montaigne consistently stresses the importance of judgment and its proper formation; the significant role which judgment plays in the composition of Montaigne's *Essais* is indicative of the heights to which man may raise himself.

BIBLIOGRAPHY

Barrière, Pierre. *Montaigne, gentilhomme français*. 2nd ed. Paris: Delmas, 1948.

Bloch, Oscar and W. von Wartburg. *Dictionnaire étymologique de la langue française*. 3rd ed. Paris: Presses Universitaires de France, 1960.

Bowman, Frank P. *Montaigne: Essays*. London: Arnold, 1965.

Brett, George Sidney. *Psychology, Ancient and Modern*. New York: Longmans, Green and Co., 1928.

Brunetière, Ferdinand. "Publications récentes sur Montaigne," *Revue des deux mondes*, XXXV (1906), 192–227.

Buffum, Imbrie. *L'Influence du voyage de Montaigne sur les Essais*. Princeton: Princeton University Press, 1946.

Cicero. *Tusculan Disputations*, trans. J. E. King, The Loeb Classical Library. London: Heinemann, 1927.

Compayré, Gabriel. *Montaigne and Education of the Judgment*, trans. J. E. Mansion. New York: Crowell, 1908.

Coppin, Joseph. *Etude sur la grammaire et le vocabulaire de Montaigne d'après les variantes des Essais*. Lille: Morel, 1925.

— *Montaigne, traducteur de Raymond Sebon*. Lille: Morel, 1925.

Cotgrave, Randle. *A Dictionarie of the French and English Tongues*. London, 1611. Reproduced from the first edition by the University of South Carolina Press, Columbia, 1950.

Cresson, André. *Montaigne, sa vie, son oeuvre*. Paris: Presses Universitaires de France, 1947.

De Man, Paul. "Montaigne et la transcendance," *Critique*, IX (1953), 1011–1022.

Dow, Neal. *The Concept and Term "Nature" in Montaigne's Essays*. Philadelphia: 1940.

Du Bellay, Joachim. *Les Regrets*. Paris: Delmas, 1955.

Estienne, Robert. *Les Mots françois selon l'ordre des lettres, ainsi qu'il les faut escrire, tournez en latin*. Nouvellement augmentez de plusieurs dictions Francoises & Latines. Paris: Nicolas Chesneau, 1572.

Frame, Donald M. "Did Montaigne Betray Sebond?," *Romanic Review*, XXXVIII (1947), 297–329.

— *Montaigne: A Biography*. New York: Harcourt, Brace & World, Inc., 1965.

— *Montaigne's Discovery of Man: The Humanization of a Humanist*. New York: Columbia University Press, 1955.

— "What Next in Montaigne Studies?," *French Review*, XXXVI (1963), 577–587.

Friedrich, Hugo. *Montaigne*. Bern: Francke, 1949.

Godefroy, Frédéric. *Dictionnaire de l'ancienne langue française et de tous ses dialectes du IXe au XVe siècle*. 10 vols. Paris: Librairie des sciences et des arts, 1937–1938.

Gray, Floyd. *Le Style de Montaigne.* Paris: Nizet, 1958.
— "The 'nouveaux docteurs' and the Problem of Montaigne's Consistency in the *Apologie de Raymond Sebond,*" *Symposium,* 18 (1964), 22–34.
— "The Unity of Montaigne in the *Essais,*" *Modern Language Quarterly,* XXII (1961), 79–86.
Hamel, S. "*Expérience-Essai*: Contribution à l'étude du vocabulaire de Montaigne," *Bulletin de la société des amis de Montaigne,* 3e série, nos. 11–12 (1959), 23–32.
Hatzfeld, Adolphe and Arsène Darmesteter. *Dictionnaire général de la langue française du commencement du XVIIe siècle jusqu'à nos jours.* 2 vols. Paris: Delagrave, 1926.
Hill Hay, Camilla. *Montaigne, lecteur et imitateur de Sénèque.* Poitiers: Société française d'imprimerie et de librairie, 1938.
Huguet, Edmond. *Dictionnaire de la langue française du seizième siècle.* Paris: Edouard Champion, 1925 to date (in progress).
— *L'Evolution du sens des mots depuis le XVIe siècle.* Paris: Droz, 1934.
Jansen, F. J. Billeskov. *Sources vives de la pensée de Montaigne: Etude sur les fondements psychologiques et biographiques des Essais.* Copenhagen: Levin & Munksgaard, 1935.
Jeanson, Francis. *Montaigne par lui-même.* Paris: Editions du Seuil, 1951.
Jones, P. Mansell. *French Introspectives from Montaigne to André Gide.* Cambridge: Cambridge University Press, 1937.
La Boétie, Estienne de. *Œuvres complètes,* ed. Paul Bonnefon. Bordeaux: Gounouilhou, 1892.
La Croix du Maine. *Les Bibliothèques françoises.* 6 vols. Paris: Saillant & Nyon, Libraires, and Lambert, Imprimeur, 1772.
Lalande, André. *Vocabulaire technique et critique de la philosophie.* 83rd ed. Paris: Presses Universitaires de France, 1960.
Lanson, Gustave. "La Vie morale selon les *Essais* de Montaigne," *Revue des deux mondes,* XIX (1924), 603–625, 836–858.
— *Les Essais de Montaigne: étude et analyse.* Paris: Mellottée, 1930.
Littré, Emile. *Dictionnaire de la langue française.* 4 vols. Paris: Hachette, 1882.
Laumonier, Paul. "Montaigne précurseur du XVIIe siècle," *Revue d'histoire littéraire de la France,* III (1896), 204–217.
Malebranche, Nicolas. *Œuvres complètes,* ed. André I. Robinet. 19 vols. Paris: Vrin, 1958–1965.
Marcu, Eva. *Répertoire des idées de Montaigne.* Geneva: Droz, 1965.
Marnix, Philippe de. *Œuvres,* ed. Albert Lacroix. 8 vols. Brussels: F. van Meenen, 1857–1860.
Matoré, Georges. *La Méthode en lexicologie.* Paris: Didier, 1953.
Merrill, Robert V. with Robert J. Clements. *Platonism in French Renaissance Poetry.* New York: New York University Press, 1957.
Micha, Alexandre. "Montaigne et le drame de l'intellect," *Mercure de France,* 303 (1948), 453–462.
Montaigne. *De l'institution des enfants,* ed. Gustave Michaut. Paris: de Boccard, 1924.
— *Essais,* ed. R. Dezeimeris and H. Barckhausen. Texte original de 1580 avec les variantes des éditions de 1582 et 1587. 2 vols. Bordeaux: Gounouilhou, 1870–1873.
— *Les Essais,* ed. Fortunat Strowski *et al.* 5 vols. Bordeaux: Pech, 1906–1933.
— *Essais,* ed. Albert Thibaudet. Paris: Gallimard, 1950.
— *Œuvres complètes,* ed. Arthur Armaingaud. 12 vols. Paris: Conard, 1924–1941.
— *Œuvres complètes,* ed. Albert Thibaudet and Maurice Rat. Paris: Gallimard, 1962.

Moore, Will G. "Montaigne's Notion of Experience," *The French Mind: Studies in Honor of Gustave Rudler*. Oxford: Clarendon Press, 1952, 34–52.

Müller, Armand. *Montaigne*. Bruges: Desclée de Brouwer, 1965.

Nicot, Jean. *Thresor de la langve françoise tant ancienne que Moderne*. Douceur, 1606. Reproduced from the 1621 edition by Picard et Cie, Paris, 1960.

Pascal. *Pensées*, ed. Léon Brunschvicg. Introduction and Notes by Ch.-M. des Granges. Bourges: Garnier, 1961.

Pasquier, Etienne. *Les Œuvres*, ed. anon. 2 vols. Amsterdam: 1723.

Peyre, Albert. *Du Prestige de la pensée*. Paris: Debresse, 1936.

Pieper, Josef. *Leisure: The Basis of Culture*, trans. Alexander Dru, with an Introduction by T. S. Eliot. New York: Pantheon Books, 1952.

Plutarch. *Moralia*, trans. Frank Cole Babbitt *et al.*, The Loeb Classical Library. 14 vols. London: Heinemann, 1927–1965.

— *Les Vies des hommes illustres*. Traduction de Jacques Amyot. Texte établi et annoté par Gérard Walter. 2 vols. Paris: Gallimard, 1937.

Poulet, Georges. *Etudes sur le temps humain*. Paris: Plon, 1950.

Rice, Eugene F., Jr. *The Renaissance Idea of Wisdom*. Cambridge: Harvard University Press, 1958.

Rolfe, John C. *Cicero and his Influence*. New York: Longmans, Green and Co., 1928.

Sacy, Sylvestre de. "Montaigne essaie ses facultés naturelles," *Mercure de France*, 315 (1952), 285–306.

Schmidt, Albert-Marie, ed. *Poètes du XVIe siècle*. Paris: Gallimard, 1953.

Seneca. *Ad Lucilium Epistulae Morales*, trans. Richard M. Gummere, The Loeb Classical Library. 3 vols. London: Heinemann, 1925.

Strowski, Fortunat. *La Sagesse française*. 4th ed. Paris: Plon, 1925.

— *Montaigne*. Paris: Alcan, 1906.

Taine, Henri. *De l'intelligence*. 13th ed. 2 vols. Paris: Hachette, 1914.

Thibaudet, Albert. "Le Quadricentenaire d'un philosophe," *La Revue de Paris*, 40 (1933), 755–776.

— *Montaigne*. Texte établi par Floyd Gray d'après les notes manuscrites. Paris: Gallimard, 1963.

Van den Bruwaene, Léon, "Les Idées philosophiques de Montaigne," *Revue néo-scolastique de philosophie*, XXXV (1933), 339–378, 489–515.

Vernay, Henri. *Les Divers Sens du mot "raison" autour de l'oeuvre de Marguerite d'Angoulême Reine de Navarre* (1492–1549). Heidelberg: Carl Winter, 1962.

Villey, Pierre. "La place de Montaigne dans le mouvement philosophique," *Revue philosophique*, CI (1926), 338–359.

— *Les Essais de Montaigne*. Paris: Nizet, 1946.

— *Les Livres d'histoire moderne utilisés par Montaigne*. Paris: Hachette, 1908.

— *Les Sources et l'évolution des Essais de Montaigne*. 2 vols. Paris: Hachette, 1908.

— *Montaigne devant la postérité*. Paris: Boivin, 1935.

INDEX

GPSR Compliance

The European Union's (EU) General Product Safety Regulation (GPSR) is a set of rules that requires consumer products to be safe and our obligations to ensure this.

If you have any concerns about our products, you can contact us on ProductSafety@springernature.com

In case Publisher is established outside the EU, the EU authorized representative is:

Springer Nature Customer Service Center GmbH
Europaplatz 3
69115 Heidelberg, Germany

Batch number: 10830943

Printed by Printforce, the Netherlands